Hudson Tuttle

Career of Religious Ideas

Hudson Tuttle

Career of Religious Ideas

ISBN/EAN: 9783337719920

Printed in Europe, USA, Canada, Australia, Japan

Cover: Foto ©Lupo / pixelio.de

More available books at **www.hansebooks.com**

CAREER OF RELIGIOUS IDEAS.

THEIR ULTIMATE:

THE RELIGION OF SCIENCE.

BY HUDSON TUTTLE,

AUTHOR OF "ORIGIN AND ANTIQUITY OF MAN," "CAREER OF THE GOD-IDEA," "CAREER OF THE CHRIST-IDEA," "ARCANA OF NATURE," ETC., ETC.

Historians of that which is, we cannot fail, except when we cease to relate the truth.—ETIENNE GEOFFROY ST. HILIARE.

How beautiful this light! it seems to beckon earth to heaven.—ALEX HUMBOLDT.

D. M. BENNETT:
LIBERAL AND SCIENTIFIC PUBLISHING HOUSE.
141 EIGHTH STREET, NEW YORK.
1878.

PREFACE.

It is time Science be heard in the discussion of man's moral relations here and immortal relations in the hereafter. Having driven metaphysics from the field of matter, it essays to enter the realm of spirit, accounting for mental and moral results by unvarying law. Over this mysterious domain exact knowledge must extend its sway. *If there is a spirit-world, it is governed by fixed laws.* If there is a spirit-existence, it must be evolved out of physical life according to determinate methods, and all moral principles must have their bases in the constitution of the world. My earnest desire is that this work may be met with the same uncompromising love of truth with which it deals with time-old theories. H. T.

RELIGION AND SCIENCE.

FUNDAMENTAL RELIGIOUS PROPOSITION.

Man was created a perfect being in a perfect world, by a direct and miraculous act of an Infinite God, and by disobedience brought sin and death into the world, thereby becoming estranged and lost from God, an uttterly depraved and fallen creature.

DEPENDENT PROPOSITIONS.

1st. As he sinned against an Infinite Being, his sin is infinite, and requires an infinite sacrifice.

2d. God, as the only Infinite Being, is alone capable of making such sacrifice.

3d. God incarnated and offered himself as such atoning sacrifice, and became a mediator between himself and sinful man to save the world.

4th. The efficacy of this mediation depends on faith.

5th. Man is a free agent, and can choose by his own free will between good and evil.

6th. Endowed with life and immortality, through the arbitrary will and for the pleasure of God, man's free choice brings on himself reward or punishment.

7th. Mortal life is a state of probation; immortality, a miraculous gift of God, for the purposes of reward and punishment.

8th. He gave the Bible as a direct revelation of his will to man, as the only and infallible guide by which lost man can be saved.

RESULTS.

A priesthood; superstition; bigotry; persecution; suppression of knowledge; and the arrogance of infallibility.

FUNDAMENTAL SCIENTIFIC PROPOSITION.

Man was evolved from lower forms of being, and has progressed from the lowest estate to his present civilization by inherent growth, and is the expression of fixed and unchanging laws.

DEPENDENT PROPOSITIONS.

1st. Man has never fallen from a state of perfection—never has been, nor can be, estranged or lost from God.

2d. The only possible mediatorship that can exist between man and God is knowledge.

3d. Sin, or evil, is imperfection, which can only be eradicated by normal growth. Man is, and must be, his own savior.

4th. A creature of organization, and subject to unchanging laws, man, in the church sense, is not a free agent, nor has he a free will. His apparent free agency is based on the combination of forces by which he became an individual.

5th. Mortal life is not probationary; immortality is not bestowed, but evolved from and a direct continuance of the physical being, by laws as sharply defined and as unchangeable.

6th. The only infallible authority is Nature rightly interpreted by Reason.

RESULTS.

Nobility of life; highest ideal aspiration for perfection; calm reliance in the presence of universal and omnipotent forces; all-embracing charity and philanthropy; an earnest and successful endeavor to actualize the ideal perfect life rendered possible by his organization.

CHAPTER I.

INTRODUCTORY.

That matter called the Christian religion was in existence among the ancients; it has never been wanting since the beginning of the human race.—*St. Augustine.*

>Change rides upon the wings of Time—
>A regal artist, dumb and still,
>Who visits God's remotest clime,
>And sculptures matter to her will.
>—*Emma Tuttle.*

History yields no example of a motive actuating man stronger than religion. To it all the most holy and sacred emotions of the heart bow in abject servitude. Love of friends, of family, of country, is as nothing compared with religious faith. The tender appeal of childhood, the fond embrace of conjugal affection, the pleading voice of fraternal ties, are at once cast aside by the devotee blind to all perception, and calloused to all the influences which usually sway the human heart. Bound to the stake, the martyr smiles at the excruciating pain, and his soul ascends in the lurid flames chanting hymns of victory. It is one of the first faculties awakened in the mind—Protean in its forms, and ever triumphant. The hero who unwavering rushes against serried ranks of bayonets, or unappalled storms the redoubt crowned with deep-throated cannon, condemned by his religion, quaking with fear, falls prostrate, and with white lips cries frantically for pardon to an offended God. Religion demands monasteries filled with monks, and convents with nuns, vowed to celibacy; and thousands rush to their lonely cells, and suffer through their mortal lives the imposition of the most revolting requirements. It asks the wife to ascend the funeral pyre of her husband, and she herself applies the torch. It asks its devotee to cast himself into the Ganges, or beneath the Car of Juggernaut, and its voice is obeyed with joy. It destroys the humanity of its recipient, transforming him into a blind fanatic, and too often an avenging fiend who will sacrifice all the human heart holds dear on the altar of its faith.

Such being its wonderful power, we ask, What is Religion?

The world gives a multitude of diverse answers. In the sense in which the word is usually employed, it means the peculiar beliefs in the form and essence of God, and the ceremonials of his worship, entertained by any particular people. In this sense it is distinct from morality, which relates to actual life. Each great race of mankind, by organization evolving a different mentality and a varying moral code, answers the question after its own manner. The Hindoo says religion consists in believing on Christna and the Holy Books, in keeping caste with the scrupulousness of olden times, observing the ceremonies prescribed, repeating long prayers, pilgrimages to holy cities and rivers, and blind obedience to the priesthood.

The Persian answers that belief in Zoroaster and the sacred Zend Avesta, the repetition of prayers, and the feeding of the sacred fires, are all essential.

The Chinese would have us believe in Confucius; the Moslem, in Mohammed; the Jew, in Moses and the Prophets. The Hindoo has his Shaster; the Persian, his Zend Avesta; the Mohammedan, his Al-Koran; the Jew, his Old Testament; the Christian, his New Testament—all claiming divine and infallible inspiration. All have their divine men —their saviors—to believe on whom is sufficient for salvation. Each has a supreme God jealous of other people's gods. Brahma, Ormuzd, Jehovah, apparently all rest on the same foundation—blind faith. Christianity is not a unit in its answer. There is a wide disparity between Catholic and Protestant, and the sects into which the latter is divided reply with countless discordant voices.

The Mother Church replies: Belief in the divinity of Jesus and the virginity of Mary, crucifixion of the body, punctual attendance at church, and hearty belief and coöperation in the forms of its fantastic worship.

The Protestants cry: Faith, grace, baptism, belief in this or that impossibility, until in the confusion it is impossible to decide. If baptism is essential, either immersion or sprinkling is wrong, and the followers of one or the other of these modes are not fulfilling God's law. If good deeds are worthless and faith is everything, those who rely on an upright life have built their house on the sands. Should good deeds prove of more avail than faith, the opposite host must eternally suffer.

All—Brahmin, Buddhist, Persian, Moslem, Jew, Catholic, Baptist, Presbyterian, Methodist, down to the smallest and most obscure sect—are equally willing to sanctify and prove their dogmas with their lives. *Martyrs are the cheapest product of mankind, and the most meaningless.* They have sealed with their blood the greatest follies with a zeal which proves nothing but their ignorance and fanaticism.

Ah, Religion! are you only a name, changeable to the varying requirements of the time—the convenience and selfishness of men? Broad and deep has been the gulf between religion and morality, and a designing priesthood has ever sought to deepen and widen it, and break down any bridge adventurous thinkers might seek to throw across. Obedience to all moral commands, unless such obedience has special reference to the Divine will, is not religion, which is "real piety in practice, consisting in the performance of all known duties to God and our fellow men, in obedience to Divine command, or from love to God and his law."

The questions arise: What is obedience? How are we to

know the will of God ? What duties do we owe to him ? What is piety ?

This definition is as broad as the world, and as narrow as the most selfish bigot can wish. It applies to the pow-wow of the Red Indian as well as to the prayers of Christians—the pilgrimage to Mecca as well as that to the Holy Sepulchre. To be religious is to observe the methods of worship of one's country. A Mohammedan may be very pious at Constantinople, but he would be an Infidel in New York. At Constantinople the Pope himself would be an Infidel dog. The pious Trinitarian does not consider the Unitarian better than an Infidel. Religion is, then, the worship of Joss-sticks—not for ourselves, but to please God.

God is a caricature. The Infinite One becomes offended and displeased if we do not sink our selfhood in him. Infinite selfishness is his predominant quality. Let oblivion conceal from the blushing day this detestable sham ! Bury deep this Christians' God, to be unearthed in future centuries, and studied as the geologist now studies the fossil monsters of the primeval time !

Out of this slough there is one method of escape—by another assertion. The Bible furnishes a code, God-given, which man must obey. This satisfies until other races produce their several sacred books, with equally positive evidence of their truthfulness; and it is learned that all the vital moral precepts were well understood before these sacred books were written, and that unless the capabilities for morality exist in the mind, there can be no revelation of moral obligations even by a God.

The religious views entertained by the Christian world are a stupendous chain of unwarrantable, insupportable, and baseless assertions. Getting lost from God, getting saved, getting nearer to God, being restored to God, and being lost from God, form a mass of verbiage, meaningless and false. Can a man be lost from an all-pervading, infinite Father ?

Not only is such a religion humiliating—it is absolutely immoral. The ceremony quickly comes to stand for the practice of virtue; the ritual takes the place of deeds ; the man is encased in impenetrable formulæ, and truth departs.

The Bible is interpreted by the sects very differently. If our eternal salvation depends on obeying the laws of God for our own sake, the choice of the sect with which we cast our fortunes, and the interpretation we accept, are fraught with momentous consequences—no less than our eternal happiness or misery. Yet are we left to stumble in darkness and doubt, and find it impossible to decide from the evidence furnished us. Whose fault is it—the Infidel's who cannot receive the evidence, or the Infinite God's who furnishes it in so imperfect a manner ? If God has made a revelation, it is because he saw its necessity, and a part of that necessity is that it must be in such a form as will be received; otherwise it answers not the ends designed, and is useless.

On the Bible, as an absolute inspiration from God, the Christian Churches found their claims. As they discard reason, they have no right to use it in determining the character of this revelation. By their acknowledgment that man cannot gain a knowledge of truth by other methods, they are compelled to base their systems on its authority. Having thus planted themselves, they one and all arrogate dictatorship in religious matters. They claim the power of commendation and denunciation. Even the most liberal in their creeds and dogmatic formulæ make this claim. They are right; all who disagree are wrong, and subjects for hell. Religion consists in belief in these peculiar tenets. The Catholic regards all Protestants as led astray by the Evil One, while the Protestant feels assured that the Catholic Church is the Scarlet Woman of Babylon. Both summarily condemn the Freethinker, the philosopher, and the scientist, as hopeless Infidels. Such is the force of education, that the arrogance of the Church has been in a measure acquiesced in, and a tacit admission of her right granted; but we ask how and when the Church received such power.

What is the Church? An aggregation of individuals for the object of religious instruction and propagation of religious ideas. The Christian Churches gather around the conception of Christ an incarnation of God. Their authority is the Bible. But the Bible nowhere even mentions a church in the modern sense. Jesus, so far from being a model of, was the antipodes of church spirit. He gathered a few fishermen around him, and taught wherever he found a willing mind to receive. He cast aside all ceremonies and rites. The observance of the Sabbath was to him an idle tale. He abolished the sacrifices, the prayer at set times and seasons, leaving only the absolute principles of morality. He bestowed no power on his disciples that the most ordinary men did not possess. The most successful missionary in his cause was one of those sent forth. Is the whole strength of argument confined to the text founding the Church on Simon Peter? Its spurious origin is too well proven to leave a doubt.

Nowhere in the Gospels has Christ sanctioned anything but pure and exalted morality. Baptism and the Supper were only accidents, and nowhere recommended as essential. Where, then, can the Church found its claims to infallible direction of the beliefs of men? Not on the Bible; not on anything Christ said or did. His life is a plain denial of all they claim.

The Church has acted from the commencement of its existence as though it held a commission from God to scourge all who opposed its exactions, and torture them into the road it said led to heaven. The Protestant sects, having lost the irresistible power of the Pope, still rely on the withering influence of excommunication, and the social pressure they wield. They cannot place the Infidel on a rack and tear his limbs to pieces, but they can torture his spirit by social ostracism, the influence of which lies in the prejudices they create.

When a thinker walks out on the breezy highlands of untrammeled thought, and would gladden the world with the spectacle of a beautiful life devoted to noble aims and lofty endeavors, how rave the sectarian winds over the theological marshlands below! and how ten thousand tongues run swift to defame his fair name! The calm soul will let them prate, as the unnoticeable anger of children.

We learn, then, that the claims of the Church to authority in matters pertaining to religion are without the least foundation. They are not sanctioned by the Gospels, nor authorized by any word or deed of Christ, but everywhere condemned. Nor can it, as an aggregation of individuals, claim authority over any individual who does not consent to such dictation. All authority thus gained is that bestowed by the brute strength of numbers.

It may be answered: These numbers are not individual aggregations, but they gather around a centre—that centre the God-man, Christ. The power of the Church arises from its holding this being as a model for human action. If Christ were a veritable incarnation—if he were God clothed in flesh—he could not be a model for finite man. His example would be useless and wholly incomprehensible. If he were simply a good and perfect man, it would be well for us to follow his example, and so would it be well to learn lessons from all exemplary men.

Thus, as a God or as a man, no power is conferred on his followers, by accepting him as a model, to enforce their views on others, or to reject what they may consider as conflicting with their established beliefs.

All authority that the Church has is that of brute power: nothing divinely delegated, but human and bestowed by might.

This right is admitted, not because it is supported by evidence, but by that blind obedience men pay to the old, which grows out of fear, admiration, and a sense of duty, the result of education.

The Church has the appliances to create fear in an eminent degree. Added to those usually attending leaders, political or theological, it holds the keys of hell and eternal damnation in its hands. The soul that bravely submits to physical torture is appalled at threats of eternal anguish. This element is chiefly relied on and is largely used in all revivals, and its thunder tones are heard in excommunications and anathemas. Mankind are loyal to their leaders, whether those leaders direct them right or wrong, and once imbued with certain notions, they are ready to sustain those leaders, from admiration of the success with which they carry forward their measures. One generation having submitted, the next is educated into submission, or, in other words, they have a sense of the moral duty of obedience.

Having by these means gained supremcy, the Church has attempted to preserve her power by two quite different methods. Thoroughly comprehending that knowledge is power, it has either sought to check its diffusion altogether, or only to disseminate such ideas as it pleased.

The universal dissemination of knowledge, it was held, was not only useless, but led to discontent, sedition, and revolution. The masses, if allowed to be informed in the arts and sciences of the ruling classes, would become turbulent and uncontrollable. The High Church party in England maintained this view until a recent date, and the supporters of slavery upheld it with most stringent laws. The other method, the deeper and more insidious, introduced by the more ultra leaders of Protestantism, and by the Jesuits into Catholicism, is to compel all to become educated, making it even compulsory with parents to instruct their children. At the same time, while opening the doors of the mind, care is taken of the mental food supplied. An injunction is served on the press and the author. No book or paper is issued until examined by the theological power, and if containing anything displeasing, it cannot appear. Authors who write in accordance with prevailing ideas are encouraged to occupy the public mind, the press thus becoming a power in the hands of the Church to disseminate its doctrines and maintain its authority. It vomits forth tracts and religious books by the million, but to every call from any conflicting idea is silent. It is not only gagged, it is made a slave, and all its giant energy compelled to labor for darkness instead of light.

The school has been supplied with books written in the service of the Church, to the exclusion of others, and every avenue to knowledge seized with rapacious hand. The primary school, the seminary, the college, if not publicly teaching theology, are controlled by theologians.

Wise and subtle as this scheme appeared, they who employed it knew not wherewith they built. The mind becomes enlarged and its perceptions sharpened even by erroneous learning. After receiving the knowledge prepared by the priesthood, it gains increased capacity; and one ray of light allowed to enter creates a desire for the whole sunshine. The New England common schools, of which those of other States are copies, were established chiefly to maintain Puritan orthodoxy; but they have in a great measure escaped from the controlling hand of the Church, and from them have flowed the heresies which have degraded its power and led to the Freethought of the present. May we soon rejoice for the day when they shall become wholly secularized, and the light of knowledge, instead of revealing the horrid machinery of theology to the ardent imaginations of the young, be allowed to shine as the sun of morning over the beauties of Nature.

Neither the Church nor any organization having the right to decide what is truth, man is thrown on his own resources for its determination. Granting the dogma of miraculous creation, every organ and function of man is designed and created for pleasure—not for pain—and it is essential that an All-wise Being make him an authority to himself. If not, how is it possible for him to receive the revelation of his Maker? Here we leave the dark nightland, where, in the miasmatic gloom of ignorance and dank vapors of superstition, theology grows like a fetid mushroom, and with relief gain the heights of untrammeled thought, where religion becomes moral obligation. Not to systems, but to the mind itself, are we to turn for the understanding of religion. The meaning of that word can be exalted. The true religious code and the moral are one. The most moral man is the most religious. Everything outside of a well-ordered life—a life devoted to the most perfect accomplishment of the object of being, under the name of whatever religion—is a sham. Religion is the citadel in which emotional ignorance has entrenched itself, and fought to the death every advance of knowledge, which, expressed in the general term of science, is the true savior of mankind.

"Ah!" it is replied, "science is well in its place, but in morals and religion it is at fault: they are beyond its pale." The worshiper of beans and garlics under the shadow of the Pyramids made the same statement four thousand years ago. Religion is the province of unreasoning faith, and the greater the faith required, the more miraculous the system and laudable the unwavering faith of the devotee. Faith is another name for credulity, and is most reprehensible.

The weapons of metaphysical theology are now useless. The war has changed its base. It has been fought on the damp marshlands of ignorance, and the combatants have been guided by will-o'-the-wisps, which they mistook for stars of heaven. Now the light of certain knowledge floods the world, and the systems of theology and metaphysics disappear. They can never change front and battle with new weapons. Knowledge not only destroys dogmatism; it renders its existence impossible. The Goliaths of theology arrayed on the battle-field of science, become phantasms, the attenuated shadows of ghosts, which amuse rather than annoy with their incoherent gibberish.

Knowledge carries men away from Churchianity. The leading minds of Europe and America stand outside of its influence. Yet they and their followers form the most moral members in their respective societies. The drifting away of the dross of dogmatism leaves the true gold of morality.

In these pages the great questions of religion and morality are treated by knowledge, and not by faith. No obscure region is covered by the "mystery of Godliness." The only mystery admitted is that of Ignorance. By religion is meant all systems, and Christianity will be weighed in the same balance with Mohammedanism, Buddhism, and the lowest Fetishism. If it stand the test, it is well; if not, why mourn? As from the mind of man has sprung all the systems of the past, he is superior to them as the master to his work, and adequate to the production of the systems essential to his future progress. The essential cannot be destroyed. Fetish gods only need to be jealously guarded.

CHAPTER II.

WHAT IS RELIGION?

The way to gain admission into the portals of science is through the portal of doubt.—*Socrates*.

He that takes away reason to make way for revelation puts out the light of both, and does much the same as if he should persuade a man to put out his eyes the better to receive the remote light of an invisible star by a telescope.—*Locke*.

If religion be devotion to and awe of personified life and intelligence, it is possessed by the brutes of the field.

> Europe, with all her nameless store
>   Of cultivation, wisdom, pride,
> Had marched through centuries of gore
>   Before she reached the lighted side
> Of God's humanity. Her veins,
>   Though pure, have run barbaric blood;
> Her fair face has worn pits and stains;
>   But change wrought error into good.
>   —*Gazelle*.

The assertion that religious phenomena are found among all races of mankind has been a standard argument to prove that man, by necessity of his organization, is a religious being, and that worship in some form is indispensable. Undoubtedly this is one of the strongest arguments possible to urge, and if received as expressing the fact that no mental phenomena can be manifested without an adequate cause residing in the mind, is indisputable. Furthermore, and a fact of great significance, religious feelings and observances become refined and elevated, and tend to disappear in morality, in exact ratio to the advance of reason and knowledge. There are shades of progress, from the Patagonian, the sum of whose religion is roasting a sea-bird's egg and singing a wild song over it, to the refined subtleties of the Evangelist.

The existence of such feelings is not a proof of their munificence, or that they should be uncontrolled. War appears normal to all mankind, and is even more universal than religion, going down through the successive grades of the animal world to the lowest. Its existence proves that man possesses combative elements in his nature, which, properly directed by reason, exert a salutary influence. It does not prove a separate faculty of war, but arises from a combination of faculties which an advanced civilization employs quite differently.

The existence of religious feelings proves no more than the love of war. We are not sure we cannot discover intimations of religion in animals themselves. When the wild winds blow, and the lightnings fill the black clouds with fire, and the air is rent with thunder, how piteously the brutes of the field fly here and there, uttering their plaintive moans, or rush into the presence of man, trembling with fear!

The first germ of religion in savage man is this same fear of the elements. Under like circumstances he cries with terror and falls prostrate, appealing for protection to something, he knows not what. Is there any difference in kind between the fear of the brute and that of the savage? The animal throws itself under the protection of man; the savage, having no visible superior to whom to appeal, personifies the elements themselves, and casts himself before the ideal of his own creation.

Those who regard man as fallen from a high estate see in the savage, not a primitive, but a degraded condition. This conclusion conflicts with the facts of human history. The races of mankind began, like the individual, ignorant and brutal. The early man was a savage, a cannibal, whose religion—if he possessed a religion—was of the grossest form. Our pride may revolt against such a view of our ancestors, but it makes it no better by denying it, and it is flattering to know that man is subject to progressive growth and unlimited achievements. Fetishism has been considered the lowest expression of religious instinct, but it does not touch the bottom of the abyss. Comte fails to meet the issue when he declares this statement insupportable. He combats a positive subject with metaphysical argument. He says if man existed in a state wholly material, there must have been "a time when intellectual wants did not exist in man; and we must suppose a moment when they began to exist, without any prior manifestation." This he concludes impossible. His argument is of that metaphysical kind, as delusive as unsatisfactory, which the author utterly discards in others. The "want" is subject to an imperceptibly slow growth. The appearance of the "want" is evidence of the prior capability for its development, and there must be a time when this development becomes manifest.

Fetishism is not the first expression of the religious sentiment. There are many species of animals in which it is apparent, especially in those which have had the advantage of the culture given by man. A kitten mistakes a ball for a living being as readily as a savage sees a life like his own in the wind. The thoughts awakened in the mind of a dog by presenting a watch to his ear are of the same kind— he regards it as a living being; the savage thinks it possessed by a demon. A Bechuana, seeing the sea and a ship for the first time, said the ship must have come of itself, for it could not have been created by man. The Yakats are represented as being so amazed by the action of a telescope in bringing distant objects close to the eye, that they believe it possessed by a spirit; writing they cannot comprehend, and books they regard as living objects that can talk.

In our own individual development we can mark the same ideas in our childhood. They even extend to our mature years; and when a machine refuses to do its work, how readily the mechanic gives it personality! The child converts a broomstick into a prancing steed, and the engineer speaks of his locomotive as a person for whom he has the warmest attachment. The child chastises the offending object; Xerxes, leading the myriads of Persia, would send a message to the turbulent sea, and bind it with chains. These are examples of the lowest Fetishism—the endowment of inanimate objects with life.

We have advanced so far from that primitive faith that we cannot study its peculiar phases without referring to people who are at present in the same stage as that which we have left in the remote distance. As human development is governed by the same unchanging laws, similar stages of growth present corresponding phenomena. As in a forest the connection between the acorn and the oak can be traced through the intermediate forms of growth, the civilized man stands connected with the savage.

This field of study is lamentably broad, as only a moiety of mankind have become what is styled civilized, and at least one-third of the human family are savages. Those vast regions forming the continents of Africa and Australia, the countless islands of the Pacific, and the interminable expanse around the North Pole, in America extending southward almost to the Great Lakes, are inhabited by rudest tribes, whose religious beliefs are of the grossest form. The Australian has not made an attempt towards embodying his religious ideas, if he has any, in rites and ceremonies. (Latham.) Certain wild songs, accompanied with gestures, mistaken for such, have proved of foreign origin. Even missionaries, eager to discover analogous ideas in the heathen they would convert, have honestly expressed their perplexity. Says one: "They have no idea of a Divine Being. They have no comprehension of the things they commit to memory. I mean especially as regards religious subjects." Another remarks: "What can we do with a nation whose language presents no terms corresponding to justice or sin, and to whose minds the ideas expressed by these words are completely strange and inexplicable?" "A kind of highly developed instinct for discovering their food which is always difficult for them to obtain, seems among them to have taken the place of most of the moral faculties among mankind," is the statement of Lesson and Garnot. Unless watched by the police, they would offend law and decency with as little scruple as the monkeys of a menagerie; and so dormant is their reason, that the same means must be employed to convince them that is used with children and idiots.

The inhabitants of Central Africa are little more advanced.

Leighton, who for four years served as missionary among the Mpongwes, Mandingos, and Grebos, important tribes, says that they have neither priests, nor idolatry, nor religious ceremonies. The testimony of Livingstone on the Bechuanas is the same. In order to translate the word God and make it comprehensible to Caffre intellect, the missionaries had to employ the word *Tixo*, meaning "wounded knee." Tixo was a well-known sorcerer, and received his name from a wound received on his knee. He was the highest ideal of the Caffre mind, and his name best translated the idea of God to their understanding.

Of the Esquimaux, people depressed by the cold as the preceding are by excessive heat, Sir John Ross speaks in no flattering terms as regards their religious status:—

"Did they comprehend anything of all I attempted to explain, explaining the simplest things in the simplest manner I could devise? I could not conjecture. Should I have gained more had I understood their language? I have much reason to doubt. That they have a moral law of some extent, 'written in the heart,' I could not doubt, as numerous traits of their conduct show; but beyond this I ould satisfy myself of nothing; nor did these efforts and many more enable me to conjecture aught worth recording. Respecting their opinions on the essential points from which I might have presumed on a religion, I was obliged at present to abandon the attempt, and I was inclined to despair.

"The Esquimaux is an animal of prey, with no other enjoyment than eating; and, guided by no principle and no reason, he devours as long as he can, and all that he can procure, like the vulture and the tiger. The Esquimaux eats but to sleep, and sleeps but to eat again as soon as he can."

South of the Himalayas, in the dense forests of Central Hindoostan, man exists in lower caste than has yet elsewhere been described. Mr. Piddington, who had extensive experience of travel, describes one of these remarkable people, whom the Hindoos call "monkey-men":

"He was short, flat-nosed, had pouch-like wrinkles in semicircles round the corners of the mouth and cheeks; his arms were disproportionately long, and there was a portion of reddish hair to be seen on the rusty black skin. Altogether, if couched in a dark corner or on a tree, he might be mistaken for a large oran-utan."

No sharp line can be drawn between man and the brute which shall leave the dawn of religious conception on one side and the absence of such on the other. The ancestors of the great European civilizations were savages as degraded as those here introduced. In the Egyptian representatives described by Champollion, the victorious Sesostris leads captive representatives of Europe, Asia, and Africa. The European is sketched as a savage clad in the skins of wild beasts, but the Syrian is attired in splendid Asiatic costume.

Europe has her own monuments to indicate the status of her ancient people.

The shell-heaps of the North, the arrow-heads and other imperishable remains found buried beneath the earth, are vestiges of peoples rude as the Red Indian of British Columbia. The inhabitants of Britain two thousand years ago met the invasion of Cæsar with arrows and spears of wood hardened in the fire. Their clothing was of skins of wild beasts, and their dwellings caves excavated beneath the earth. It is well determined that these savages, shouting their harsh war-cries as they gallantly met in unequal combat the invincible legions of Rome, have absorbed their conquerors, and that the present English people are their direct descendants.

This progress has involved an equal advance in religious conceptions. Every increment of knowledge threw new light on the nature and influence of the gods, and revealed more correctly the relations of man to his fellows. There is not a vestige of moral sense until the intellect is capable of comprehension.

Religion is the observance of certain ceremonies. Why are these observed? Because they are supposed to have been dictated by the gods, and especially pleasing to them. They propitiate their wrath and win their favor. Wholly selfish are they, springing from fear of the gods. The gods are never angry; and, although man for immemorial ages has sought their favor by prostration and sacrifice, in no instance have they interfered with the established order of things.

The religious element is *fear*, by which the imagination is perverted and reason enslaved. This is its ultimate analysis.

It is said, we are conscious of this element within us—that, by the failure of our schemes, the blasting of our hopes, the mystery which gathers round our lives, the limitation of our understanding, the unfathomableness of causation, we are prone to bow in submission, and acknowledge a superior Power governing Nature.

But we find, as knowledge of the laws of causation becomes more accurate, we are enabled to account for the blasting of our hopes, the failure of our plans, the mystery of our lives—are less impressed and overwhelmed with a sense of the unknown, and feel less of that dependence which some acute metaphysicians claim to be the ultimate of religious feeling. Here the distinction is drawn between morality and religion. The observance of the prescribed ceremonials of his time has constituted the religious man, and no amount of good works could shield him from the charge of infidelity if he neglected such observances. Moral ideas are not naturally allied to religious, and flow from a different source. To primitive man the observance of superstitious customs is far more essential than moral conduct. Cherishing the coarsest vices, he will suffer death before he will disobey the requirements of superstition.

CHAPTER III.

HISTORICAL REVIEW.—FETISHISM.

If any man love acorns since corn is invented, let him eat acorns; but it is very unreasonable that he should forbid others the use of wheat.

Savage man is depressed and overpowered by the objective world. He is the sport and buffet of the elements. The invisible wind, bearing on its wings clouds and tempest, through whose chambers the lightnings are flung and thunders bay; the ever-moving waters of river and sea; the sunshine flooding the earth—are grand and inexplicable mysteries to his feeble mind. He endows all objects with life; fires arrows to intimidate the lightning; undertakes hostile expeditious against offending winds; or shouts his battle-cry to frighten the monster devouring the eclipsed moon. Every moving thing has life and intelligence like his own. The animal world forms one great family, of which he is the elder brother. They understand each other and him. Like a child he converses with them. "Do not cry like a woman, but bear death like a brave," says the Indian to the wounded bear. "He keeps silent for fear of slavery," says the Negro of the baboon. His ardent imagination, unrestrained by reason, exalts the instincts of his brother animals. He is not far removed from them, and, astonished at their sagacity and the mystery of their instinctive actions, believes them his superiors.

He worships, because he fears, everything—rocks, trees, streams, mountains, sun, and stars. These are worshiped direct, and not as types or symbols of inferior deities, as is often claimed, for the mind at this stage is not capable of any conception beyond the sphere of the senses. The object was worshiped as a god, not God behind a veil. Each individual, according to his caprice, selected an object of worship ; at first only for a time, but afterwards for a longer period, even during life. Objects exciting fear, terror, or emotions of pleasure, were first selected. The savage is ruled by the passions. He cannot be said to reason. He is controlled by his emotions. He worships that which he most fears, or from which he expects the greatest assistance. His motive is fear. The dark is a monster—every obscure cavern, the jaws of destruction. Terrified by the life he cannot comprehend, he personifies that life ; and coming to a belief that personalities stand behind visible effects, a sense of his own helplessness intensifies his fear. He believes these personalities interfere in the affairs of men, and may be influenced by prayers and incantations. He devoutly believes in witchcraft and sorcery. In this early theology, morality has no part. The gods do not interfere for the purpose of rewarding man's moral or punishing his immoral acts, for he has not arrived at the understanding of moral relations.

His dim consciousness of a future state is fraught with terror. Death, the surrender of existence to the elemental forces, is a frightful phenomenon to primitive man. The spirit then leaves the body, to wander an unseen shade, capable of assuming any shape, and inflicting torments on the living. Its name must not be pronounced, for fear of recalling it. The world of spirits is terrible from its invisibility; and the savage, fearless in battle with overwhelming foes, feels utterly powerless and prostrates himself before the mysterious and irresponsible beings of the air.

To enter this invisible world and subject its shades to mortal will—to approach the gods in their secret chambers, and engage them in the furtherance of mortal plans—has been from earliest times the daring scheme of theology.

This is its basis, from which the most enlightened notions of antiquity did not arise. It is encouraged by Catholicism in holy relics, the cross, rosaries, and amulets; and by the Protestant in holy days and books. The metaphysical philosophers, when they assign a soul to Nature, and lose themselves in a bewildering Pantheism, return to Fetishism.

Here is the cradle of theology. It exists in its intensest form. The savage, by deifying all objects, dwells constantly in the presence of his gods. He cannot escape from them. He illustrates a state theologians never weary of applauding, wherein reason creates no doubt, nor examines with too curious eye the vague theories of cosmology. All ideas are theological. Every act of man's life has direct reference to his theological belief. There is no necessity for mediators between him and them, and priests are not serviceable. He appeals directly to his gods. There is no religious system, as each individual creates his own. All is indeterminate, vague, and unreal. When everything is regarded as subject to the caprice of controlling intelligences, there can be no conception of universal law or fixity of action. The spirit of investigation is dormant, or overwhelmed by the religious emotions. It is for this reason the Fetish state is one of intellectual stagnation, and progress out of it is extremely slow. The mind is so preoccupied with its childish vagaries as to preclude correct observation. When Nature becomes thus idealized, there is no room for human effort. The gods rule arbitrarily, and nothing is left for man but to appease their anger or flatter their vanity by abject homage. Such conceptions cannot exert an elevating influence. They rather impede progress, and suffocate thought by superstition—the childish fear of evil beings. Man travels a long and weary road, one *directly* diverging from religion, before he gains the mastery of nature, and through moral sensibilities recognizes a benevolent being as Creator. This early condition has not yet been wholly outgrown, and too often is the spectacle presented of men of scientific acumen prejudiced by religious dogmatism.

To understand the feelings and ideas of savages, we must place ourselves in their position. Standing on the high ground of the present, we find it difficult to appreciate their sensations; but if we imbibe the true Fetish spirit, we shall be astonished that infant man, placed in a strange world, which appeared to him like a gigantic phantasmagoria, was not led into greater errors by his theories, founded as they were on illusions instead of correct observation. It is usual for theologians to regard the systems of Paganism as impostures, and their priests as jugglers; but no fact is more patent than that all these systems are legitimate outgrowths of the mind, and these jugglers are the parents of the present race of theologians. The Puritans were shocked at the pow-wows of the Indians, referring them to the Devil; but the Indians were undoubtedly as sincere as the rigid Puritans. Theological ideas are born of the necessities of their time. Artifice and dissimulation may answer immediate ends, but they can never be received by whole races of men. Those whom it is customary to regard as impostors were thoroughly convinced themselves, and found responsiveness in those they led. The dreadful extravagances into which they fell are sufficient proof of their own entire sincerity.

The worship of plants and animals may have served a beneficial purpose before their usefuness could be learned. The savage is intent on destruction alone, and without some check might destroy himself by thoughtlessly exterminating the animals which supplied him with food. Each selects an object for his own individual worship—a tree, an animal, a rock, a stream—and addresses his prayers direct. Any uncommon occurrence—as an earthquake, tornado, or falling meteor—attracts general attention, and from many elicits homage. A black stone became the shrine of, or rather at first *was*, Cybele. Rough blocks of stone, from some singularity of form, were worshiped by the ancient people of Greece. The glory of the rising sun—the activity of life evoked by its presence—the calm repose of his going down, are among the most surprising events of Nature. The splendor of the starry hosts of night, if not as startling, is full of awful mystery. The sun, as source of life, is chief among the gods, and the stars are living souls. When blind adoration advanced to star-worship, the borders of Polytheism were reached. The Fetish of the individual became that of his family; when the family enlarged to a tribe, it became that of the tribe; and as it still enlarged by growth or conquest, it became the chief of the nation's gods. During this growth the conception of the Fetish changed. The object was no longer worshiped, but a spirit behind the object. A generalization was made by the worshiper. It was no longer an individual tree he adored, but the Spirit of all the trees; not the brook, or sea, but the Spirit of all the waters; not the different winds, but the god of the wind.

A part of Fetishism was the Phallic worship which lies at the foundation of all religions, and is among the oldest faiths. The mysterious process of creation, typified by the male and female organs of generation, the *phallus* and *yoni*, early attracted the attention of savage man. He worshiped the symbols of those organs, called his gods by their names, and invented rites and appropriate ceremonies. The bull, the horse, the ram were taken for symbols, and the sun, source of all creation, was worshiped as the chief god.

The unity of god grew out of the worship of the *yoni*, while the trinity developed from the devotion to the triple character of the male organs, or phallus. Hindostan furnishes an illustration of this early faith, and the ideas connected therewith. The phallus became the cross, emblem of eternal life, spiritualized from the type of material creation.

With this enlargement of their spheres, the character of the beings worshiped changes, becomes spiritualized, yet transcendentally human. The Anthropomorphism is not lost for a moment; it is constantly magnified. The gods are removed from man by the intervention of physical objects —by whole provinces of physical objects. They become active forces. The necessity of a mediator to interpret their will becomes felt, and priests are introduced. The medicine-man of the Indian, the juggler of the African, are illustrations of the early priesthood. They, by observing certain customs, more or less absurd, come in nearer contact with their deities. They can avert evil, bring rain, make the chase or war-path successful, assist their friends, or overwhelm their enemies.

At first they have little power, but they soon come to be feared as much as the gods whom they interpret. As love of power is a dominant motive with man—and especially on this low plane, they were not tardy in grasping any means and putting forth their strength. They surrounded their gods with mystery, invented ceremonies, sacrifices, and forms innumerable, by which the gods were removed beyond contact with common people, and their own office rendered more necessary. By keeping the people in profound ignorance they made them willing dupes, and from age to age strengthened the power of theology. It became tyrannical, usurped political as well as spiritual dictatorship, and at times rested on the prostrate nations like a horrid vampire, paralyzing their strength and crushing every effort of advancement.

Fetishism with our own race is of the remote past, yet its stain is indelibly fixed on our religious system. Christianity is full of it. Claiming, as it does, divine completeness and the worship of the one true God, there would be little left of it were its Fetishism stripped away. When pestilence smites our cities, the earthquake prostrates their proud towers in ruins, or storms devastate, prayers and sermons are sent forth from every Christian pulpit asking God to deal lightly, or charging these natural events to warning Providence. In seasons of drought, fasts are still held to invoke rain, in exactly the same spirit in which the Indian medicine-men shake their calabashes and call on the Great Spirit. Churches are peculiarly holy places, Sunday a holy day, and fasts, penance, and the sacrifice of worldly considerations peculiarly acceptable to God. The outbursts of the elements, in the Christian view, are acts of Providence. Recently the Californian earthquake-called out an expression from clergy and laymen honorable to Fetish worshipers. Instead of seeing the activity of volcanic forces in the subterranean axis on which that country is placed, they saw only the warnings of an angry God. It would be difficult to say why California needs such warning more than New York, where the revenue of the most aristocratic church is derived from the rent of its estate occupied as drinking saloons, gambling hells, and houses of prostitution—whose sleek, high-salaried minister is literally clothed by the activity of the purple fingers of starvation, and fed by the sale of human souls.

The annual Thanksgiving ordered by the American Government, and reëchoed by the States, is a relic of Fetishism, and, as such, is degrading in its tendencies. It is a hopeful sign that year by year the "Proclamation" is becoming little more than a form, and we may hope, at no distant day, a chief magistrate may be elected having sufficient manhood to ignore this absurd and outgrown custom.

The lingering faith in miracles is a remnant of the belief that the gods manage everything. Miracles are at the foundation of all systems of religion; and it is maintained by leading theologians that the human mind is so constituted that it cannot believe religion of divine origin unless accompanied with miracles. Catholicism retains the miracle-working power, which its priests continue to practice, and the erudite Protestant divine stands up in his pulpit, a competitor with the African rain-maker. This belief is like some molluscs, found fossil in the rocks of all past ages, and with charmed lives flourishing in the seas of the present: it grasps the animal and emotional faculties, and, as long as they are in ascendancy, will not yield its tenacious life.

Polytheism constantly presents its Fetish origin. The family or tribe Fetish became the Panates of the Romans and the bull Apis of the Egyptians; the national Fetish, the Olympian Jove of Greece—the Capitoline Jupiter of Rome—the Caaba of Arabia.

It would be presumed that the Jews from the earliest period, carefully instructed by the only true God, would not show the least trace of religious progress, for their system was not of growth but revelation. Contrary to this inference—and infallibly indicating its human origin—they present all phases of growth, and, at the period of their greatest splendor, Fetishism and Polytheism blended with their vaunted Monotheism. The Seraphim of Laban was a family Fetish; the horses consecrated to the Sun in the Temple of Solomon (2 Kings xxiii, 2) were of the tribe, and the Cherubim and Most Holy Place were national Fetishes. The God of Abraham was a coarse Fetish. The Jews never escaped the influence of grossest idolatry. They believed that their Jehovah dwelt especially in the Holy Place of their Temple, and propitiated him by sacrifices, rites, and ceremonies innumerable. He is a mean, cruel, unjust, vindictive, blood-thirsty despot, to whom the purely human and lovable Jove of Greece must not be compared. The Jews reflected their own stern, grim, and revengeful natures in their God, and their religion nowhere indicates a superhuman origin.

Fetishism is emphatically a religion of fear, because it reflects most clearly the origin of what are called the religious feelings. It asserts the anger of the gods, and its priests are tireless in their efforts to invent methods by which they can be appeased. They run wild with a terrible hallucination. The more unnatural an action, the more pleasing to the gods. Mutilation—as cutting off a finger, knocking out a tooth, flagellation, sacrifices—often human—are required of the servile devotee. Knowledge is repressed. All ideas of fixed order or law are lost in creation resolved into a succession of miracles. As these are not always in accordance with the welfare of man, appropriate gods are assigned to each. Classes of gods are formed—one good, the other evil. Man becomes a buffet between the two. Sacrifice gains the favor of the first, and appeases the anger of the last. There is God-worship and Devil-worship—as illustrated in the Christian Church, which assigns in its theology the second place to the God of Evil.

The later phase of Fetishism—where every individual has his own particular object of worship—so far from exerting a moral influence, acts in the opposite direction. It loosens the moral bonds, if any exist, and the possession of the especial favors of a god makes its recipient selfish and overbearing. If the Fetish united the members of the tribe in closer union, it intensified their hostility to other tribes. The national Fetish would become jealous of those of others, and all wars would become religious crusades—the national Fetishes commanding and guiding their followers. The jealousy of the Fetishes or gods, arrays tribe against tribe—nation against nation. The words "foreigner" and "enemy" become synonymous. War becomes the normal state of mankind, and the slaughter of nations acceptable sacrifice to the gods, who love the steaming blood of their enemies. This instinct of destruction at times becomes so energetic that the life of the worshiper is jeopardized, the necessities of the sacrificial altar obligating incessant war to secure captives to appease the anger of the terrible gods. The Aztecs carried this slaughter to such excess that often in default of captives they drafted from their own ranks, and from this cause the nation was rapidly declining. The Jews furnish an appalling example of a people blindly obeying the commands of their Fetish as interpreted by their priests. Jehovah is a god of battles —commands the extermination of whole nations; the butchery of men, women, and children; the prostitution of the charms of woman ; and countless unmentionable horrors. When the battle thickens, he guides the shafts of death, and even consents to stay the course of the sun to allow his butchers to accomplish their demoniac task. Only among the cannibals of the South Sea is there a parallel example. The sacred historian has recorded the slaughter of the Midianites, the dispossession of the comparatively refined and opulent Canaanites, with a heartlessness equaled only by the fiendishness of the commands of Jehovah.

The political influence of such a religion is to encourage a narrow, intense patriotism, and exclusive national isolation. It institutes two codes—one for the stranger, the other for citizens—a distinction retained by the Jews.

Fetishism evolves Polytheism by insensible degrees, and the two are inextricably blended. The worship of the object is transferred to the spirit, but to the very latest the image is preserved, and the Polytheist bestows quite as much adoration on the one as on the other.

CHAPTER IV.

HISTORICAL REVIEW—POLYTHEISM.

Who does not see that the abyss becomes every day deeper under the belief of the past, and that science at a given moment will become the foundation of more perfect morality?—
POUCHET.

THE primary claim of theology is that man could not have attained a true religion without a revelation. Plunged in idolatry, he could not have extricated himself, but would have sunk deeper and deeper without such divine guidance. The Old Testament accomplished little for the Jew, and the New produced no sudden effect. There was steady but slow growth from Fetishism to Anthropomorphism, and the transition from Paganism to Christianity was an almost imperceptible change. Such must be; for the gods being projections of the minds of their worshipers, change with their mental growth. The reception of a superior god presupposes superiority in the recipient. Metaphysical speculation on the character and origin of the gods of Polytheism belong to an age long subsequent to their active worship. The devotees have no attenuated theories of godly existence, else they would be philosophers, and not devotees. All the fine theories by which writers have sought to involve ancient mythology in allegory and fable only show how little their authors entered into and comprehended ancient life. Apollo was not the sun to his worshipers, but a godlike man. Zeus was not the sky, but a man who ruled the sky. There was no allegory, no mystic meaning, to the early worshipers. A deity stands behind the object and receives homage. As the intellect commenced its grand self-analysis, purely intellectual conceptions began to be deified. The confusion which has arisen in the study of mythology is the result of its reception as a whole, and not as a production of successive advances. It would be as accurate to speak of the fossils of geology as a whole, without distinguishing the ages to which they belong.

The gods are the active energies of the world, while matter is inert and passive to their will, a doctrine which has been almost universally held until the present conception of "force" as the energizing power inherent in matter As the human mind cannot conceive of the existence of a higher type than itself, the gods must be human in all their qualities. Even the Olympian Jove was human in passions, emotions, and desires. The gods are born and nourished, are married and become parents, but are immortal and never grow old. They gather around the festive board in Olympus, quaff nectar, and partake of celestial food. The Polytheist dwelt in a charmed world. Every object breathed poetry. He was an especial ward of the gods, some of whom, go where he would, he was sure to meet. Pluto, Neptune, and Jove divided between them the domains of the nether world—the ocean, the land, and sky. The sun and moon had their deities. Ceres brings the harvest; the Muses inspire the golden tongue of Poesy; Mars drives the chariot of war. Every act of life or occupation has especial deities ; every nation has its chief god: Zeus, Athena, Juno, Baal, Osiris, Jehovah, Odin—partial to their particular people, and more powerful than the gods of others. These chief gods, possessing human propensities, can be tempted at times to transfer their power to other nations. Jacob made a bargain with Elohim, and the Romans prayed the gods of other nations to join their conquering standard. When nations fought, it was rather to test the strength of their respective gods rather than their own. When the conquerors forced their religion on the conquererd, it was rejected until it was determined whether the defeated gods were only temporarily banished to caves or mountains, or overthrown. The Romans adopted the conquered gods into their Pantheon, but the Aztecs shut them up in a temple for that purpose.

The apotheosis of great and good men intensified the anthropomorphic conceptions of the gods. Men who serve their nations in important and critical missions—overthrowing their enemies, or introducing ameliorating improvements—receive the worship of their grateful countrymen, and are enshrined with the gods. As the Semite was overawed by the dim sense of an overruling power received from the sameness of the deserts inhabited by that race, the early Greeks or Pelasgians were impressed in a manner exactly opposite by the diversity Nature presented. Of quick sense and fancy, deeply sympathizing with the external world, they, out of the exuberance of their own life, imparted that principle to every object. Nothing was inert or lifeless. The teeming earth, the rushing winds, the wild clouds, the grand mountains, the glorious sun, the moon and stars—all by their motions manifested life. They felt not so much awe, as affection and kinship with Nature. Savages they were, but savages with fine fancy. They gave names to the elements, and at first had no conception of an individuality separate from them. Then, in process of growth, the moving power was referred to intelligence, but that intelligence preserved the former name. Zeus, or Deus— the upper air, or the sky, when personified and made a god, retained the name of the celestial regions. He it was who dwelt on the summits of mountains and drew clouds around him as a mantle. As the Supreme Deity, the gods of inferior position gathered in a great family around him, quaffing ambrosia and feasting at his table. His nod is the unchangeable decree of Fate, and his eternal serenity can by no means be disturbed. The fixed order and succession of events are his, and from him all power is primarily derived. The Greeks were worshipers of Nature. Their deities were human—immortal—but requiring food, and the savor of sacrifice was agreeable to them. They loved, hated, were jealous and capricious, and often involved Jove himself in their quarrels.

As soon as the gods became anthropomorphic, they interested themselves in the affairs of men. Their aid could be procured by prayer, but not with certainty. The most exalted hero might innocently provoke their implacable anger. They were offended when mortals forgot, in the intoxication of success, their own weakness, and claimed equality with themselves. But uninterrupted success, even meekly borne, was odious. "I know the invidiousness of fortune; your extraordinary prosperity excites my apprehensions," said Amasis, King of Egypt, to Polycrates, whose friendship he therefore renounced. Minor afflictions were courted by the prosperous as satisfying the gods, and thus averting greater calamities. The deities were always pleased with rites and ceremonies performed for their own especial benefit, and these were so important that even their involuntary omission received terrible retribution. Natural law and the fixed order of events have no place in this system: the gods act arbitrarily. Theology explains everything after the manner of the Mohammedan, who says earthquakes are due to the cow throwing the world from one horn to the other; or the Muycas, who say the world-supporting god wearies, and changes his burden from one shoulder to the other. In the progressive growth of ideas, a unitizing power is found in a chief god, who reflects the highest ideal of the worshiper. The chief god is absolute and perfect, yet his omnipotence and perfection are limited by finite conceptions. Zeus has his weakness, and Jehovah is a narrow despot. The way is slowly prepared for Monotheism by the dependency of the lesser gods on one all-powerful chief. The amenability of even this god to law—the shadowing forth of what is now absolute Science—is expressed in a sentence of Herodotus: "It is impossible even for God to escape Fate." This state of ignorance and childishness was the paradise of the priesthood; for Catholicism truly says: "Ignorance is the mother of devotion." The medicine-man advanced with swift strides to supremacy in the State; he unscrupulously grasped power in any and every form and exerted it in a remorseless manner. The intellectual activity of Greece escaped in the exuberance of its youthful vigor the servile obedience to the priestly caste, but on other nations it has been the veritable Old Man of the Sea, clutching and holding fast. Their history is written in blood—a history of the most atrocious crimes and terrible misery the world can ever produce. No outrage on Nature, no corruption of the human mind, has been sufficiently appalling to satisfy the demands of priestly theology.

By pretending to the occult knowledge of astrology and divination, they seemed to the credulous masses to hold the keys of fate in their hands. They monopolized learning, and the most superficial knowledge of physical science was of invaluable service to them in an age of ignorant credulity. Accurate observations of the weather, enabling its changes to be predicted, the adroit management of poisons in an age when their symptoms were not understood, have made the reputation of many a prophet. The priesthood has generally surrounded itself with the awful mysteries of self-sacrifice, renouncing the world, dwelling in cells in their temples little better than dungeons, observing series of fasts, vigils, penance, ablutions, flagellations, and tortures, often becoming more fanatical than those they led.

Being the only learned class they have always sought—and generally with success—to seize all the means of education. Understanding the plasticity of the young mind and the ineradicability of ideas once firmly fixed, they have craftily moulded the minds of youth to their wills, and secured from the matured man abject and unquestioning reverence for their religion. They have, on the other hand, served a purpose for good. They have nourished the arts and sciences so far as comported with their advantage; they were for continuous ages the only educated class. Levying tithes in the names of their gods, the priesthood becomes free from want, and their whole attention directed to study and contemplation. They wield their subtle influence over the ruling classes, and form the power behind the throne. The will of the gods, expressed through the priestly oracle, is of greater potency than the united voices of the people. Their "Thus saith the Lord" becomes the watchword of unspeakable crimes and tyranny. They have been regarded as necessary to the progress of the race most falsely, for the race has advanced in antagonism to its spiritual rulers; they have been a dead lock on the wheels. Whenever and wherever they have been in the ascendancy, the nation thus controlled has sunk in decay, and, prematurely old, become the vassal of stronger powers. Egypt furnishes an extreme example, attaining great perfection in that knowledge encouraged by the priesthood, but becoming stagnant and effete. Hindoostan is another, showing the lethargy induced by theocratic rule. Rome was not repressed by its influence; and Greece, freest of all ancient nations, attained the highest civilization. The priesthood is necessary, as it is necessary for early man to be a cannibal; but it cannot from this be argued that the latter is necessary to progress. Cannibalism in some instances has almost destroyed savage peoples, and, pressed into the service of the gods, it has produced—as in Mexico—deplorable results, blasting the nascent civilization there springing up. While those nations over which the priesthood has wielded the most undisputed power have fallen into the lethargy of death, in exact ratio as others have escaped such influence has been the nobility of their civilization. Greece, most emancipated from theocratic rule, shines like a star amidst the darkness of ancient night. Her band of freethinkers bore aloft the ægis of intellectual life and handed it down to the present through the flood of Roman conquest and theocratic barbarism of the Middle Ages. In her free atmosphere, where the ceremonials of worship were celebrated by the father for his household, or the prince for his people, a class of men arose—the philosophers—impossible in a nation governed by a theocracy, who, free from all authority, pursued the studies of art, literature, and science, and blessed all succeeding ages of the world.

The morality of Polytheism was greatly superior to that of Fetishism. It shows either gross ignorance or wilful misstatement to pronounce the ancients, prior to the advent of Christianity, wanting in morality. The lives of some of their great men are comparable with any of those of modern times. The philosophers of Greece and Rome taught that sin was a disease, and virtue health of the spirit—that perfection should be the aim, and all should endeavor to live divine lives. Never have the duties of man been more clearly set forth. The theocracy separated religion from morality, and the observance of the routine of sacrifices and ceremonies came to stand for a well-ordered life, just as it does under the Monotheistic system of the present. It has been truly said that Rome, conscious of her strength and destiny, worshiped herself. The larger part of her festive days were commemorative of great events in her annals, rather than devoted to special duties. The eagles of her conquering legions were sacred, and the altar was placed in the centre of the camp as the Ark of God was in that of the Israelites. Rome deified and erected temples to her virtues. Concord, Faith, Constancy, Modesty, Hope, and Peace had their respective votive shrines. The deification of these virtues indicates the noble aspirations of their devotees, and the constant presence of their gods must have produced a salutary effect.

The gods, though dwelling on high Olympus, possessed domains on the earth, held in the same regard as those of the king, distinguished by an altar protected by a sacred grove. Temples were erected on these holy grounds, which were often cultivated for the maintenance of the ceremonies prescribed by their possessors and of the priests. Every trade had its presiding deity, as it now has its patron saint. There was a god to protect the traveler, the sage, and the warrior. The influence of a firm belief in such divine presence, cannot in this age be appreciated. That it was implicitly believed, and even to a late day, there can be no doubt. In the age of the Antonines the Attic husbandman believed in the power of the hero of Marathon, and the Arcadians could hear the pipings of Pan. The belief of the common people was a religious faith. National misfortunes, by making them cling with greater affection to the past, strengthened the influence of the old faith.

The religion of the ancients was not deficient in elements of fear. It was not an easy system, presenting no punishment for sin, but gave positive assurance that no wrongful thought or action could escape its consequences. The messengers of the gods, the Furies, by the terror they awakened, placed on the actions of mortals the restraint of fear. Homer wraps them in dreadful obscurity, places their dwelling in the awful depths of the invisible world, and makes them horrible to the gods whose mandates they execute. Shrouded in darkness, they go forth on their errands, and by no means can they be propitiated. Stern, inevitable retribution for crime was theirs. Sooner or later, with soft but swift steps, they overtook the guilty, and no prayer or sacrifice could loosen their remorseless hands. Absolute and eternal justice was their goal.

Not beliefs but actions reveal the moral status of a people Man's ideas of God have very little influence on his practical morality. A Catholic, a Deist, or an Atheist may entertain equally elevated moral views. The idea of God is rather an effect than a cause. The great sects—Brahmins, Buddhists, Moslems, and Christians—entertain conceptions of God and have a standard of morality evolved from the circumstances peculiar to each, and the worshiper at one shrine is as often an upright, honest man as at another. The better the individual, the higher and purer his moral conceptions and intellectual aspirations, the more exalted and refined his ideal personification. If the negation of Atheism is reached, the manly boldness which denies the received dogmas of the time is a guarantee of an upright mind. Atheists are notable for uprightness of character. The idea of God presented by others may have its effect on those who receive it, but not on its originators.

Polytheism, in its highest form, led to a cheerful acceptance of the good and ill of life, and enjoyment of present blessings. Religion was joyous, and rarely made unreasonable demands on its receivers. The Sacred Mysteries absorbed religious fervor, and through symbol'c ceremonies became a strong tie, binding its votaries together, and a teacher of all the noble virtues and manly living. They were the embodied conceptions of sages and poets, of the future life, the characters of the gods, and the soul's transition to them. The secrets of the greater mysteries were so carefully preserved that little is known of the grand philosophy of life they sought symbolically to impress on the trembling initiate, but enough is known to show how deeply early Christianity imbibed its forms and philosophy.

The popular belief in immortality among the Greeks differed little from that of the early Christians. Names changed, but the ideas remained the same. The spirit at death at once entered Hades, but it enjoyed no rest until its funeral rites were properly performed. It was as important that the body of the slain hero be recovered as that the battle be won, and the most desperate contests occurred over the fallen. In the Under-world they pursue occupations the same as on earth, only like phantoms. They have no strength ; this they receive by means of the blood of victims sacrificed by living friends ; then they regain memory and affection for a time, and recognize and feel for those they have left on earth. The vast multitude in Hades are in a stupified, half-conscious state. While the shades of heroes and sages were transported to an island in the ocean, exempt from all the vicissitudes of the seasons, and perpetually fanned by cool and fragrant western breezes, the enemies of the gods were removed to the abyss of Tartarus, as far beneath Hades as that was beneath the earth. Its iron door shut them from the mercy of the offended gods; its brazen floor was pressed by the footsteps of never-ending toil; and its vaulted arches echoed the groans of never-satisfied longings. This poetical conception was afterwards refashioned into the loathsome Purgatory of Catholicism.

Sacrifices often were enacted poems, visible expressions of gratitude to the unknown and incomprehensible forces of Nature. Out of awe grew a sense of dependence, and the performance of a given labor was as nothing without the approval of the gods. Libations were made at the social meal; the harvest gave its offerings; the youth and maiden gave votive locks to certain deities. Simple rites were these, but satisfying. The earliest sacrifice was made to appease the anger or court the favor of the invisible powers, and when the anthropomorphic ideas strengthened, the earthly ruler became the image of the gods, and what to him was pleasing was regarded so to them. They were envious, and must be appeased by costly presents and rich banquets. The costliness of these was in proportion to the supposed displeasure of the gods. This belief carried to extreme would require the life of man as the greatest sacrifice. The immolation of the twelve Trojans by the Greeks on the funeral pyle of Patrocles to sooth his departed soul, of two Greek and two Gallic captives by the Romans when the gods through Hannibal threatened the life of their city, the fate of Jephthah's daughter, and the command to Abraham to offer up his son, and the sacrifice every fifth or seventh month by many ancient peoples of a victim chosen by lot, indicates the universality of this belief.

Polytheism is accused of worshiping images for gods, but no one acquainted with its genius can for a moment entertain the idea that the humble worshiper regarded the image as anything more than a bond between himself and the deity it represented. He had outgrown this early belief, yet his mind, unable to grasp the conception of the gods, employed images as assistants. Some nations discarded artificial images, and with keen intellectual perception paid direct homage to the life-giving sun and the starry hosts. The Jews discarded images, but, by concealing their deity behind the veil of the Temple and creating an awful mystery, before the veil of which they knelt, were as real idolaters as the surrounding peoples.

Polytheism taught a narrow patriotism founded on the partial and exclusive character of its national gods, comprised in the love of country and hatred of foreigners. This exclusiveness was subdued by the conquests of Alexander and policy of Rome, whereby nations were brought into direct contact and amalgamated. The comparison of the gods assembled in the Pantheon prepared the way for the reception of Monotheism. The multitudes of gods were amenable to the control of the One God. This was not a new theory, but rather the sweeping away of old poetic garniture of subsidiary deities. When the apostle spoke of the Unknown God, he was readily understood by the Athenians. Monotheism was a direct growth of Polytheism, but various deflections were made on the way as various obstacles to growth were interposed. Of these, Dualism and Pantheism are the most important. The belief in a supremely good and a supremely evil being antedates the birth of Zoroaster. Involving a contradiction, it has been one of the most annoying and perplexing problems, over which to this day the Christian world wrangles. Two infinite and supreme beings cannot exist; hence it was taught that the evil god, once good, had fallen from his high estate. But an infinite being cannot change. The evil god must be less in power than the good god, and if the latter is all-powerful and good he could not allow the evil one to exist. The Persians solved this problem by referring both as emanations from one source, which Supreme Fountain became identical with the One, and Dualism ran its course. This belief, through the Eastern disciples, entered early Christian theology, and has ever since made it a system of Dualism instead of Monotheism. The Persian god of evil, Siva, became Satan, and has acted a most conspicuous part in the religion of the Christian world. Even at present his name is pronounced in the pulpit quite as frequently and with as much unction as that of God.

Pantheism regards Creation as God. It was a favorite theory of the ancient philosophers, who advocated both its material and spiritual form. Creation is the result of the laws inherent in matter itself. Nothing is fortuitous; all change is by the fixed fiat of law. God is the sun of Nature. Spiritual Pantheism is based on a metaphysical dream. God is the sun of the Spirit, from whom every *thing* is evolved. He is ever the same, yet constantly unfolding into new forms. God *only* possesses substantiality. He becomes self-conscious only through man. This mystical docrine is capable of many changes, and bewilders and deludes by seeming to present tangible ideas when it presents only dreams.

CHAPTER V.

HISTORICAL REVIEW—MONOTHEISM.

In all departments, progress for the Indo-European people will consist in departing farther and farther from the Semetic spirit. . . . Our religion will become less and less Jewish.
RENAN.

CONFINED to narrow limits, and numerically insignificant compared with the other leading races, the Semite has made a deep influence both for good and for evil on the destinies of the world. It was first to engage in commerce, and invent a phonetic alphabet, which, more than any one cause, by the facilities it affords for the preservation of ideas, has tended to elevate mankind. From it sprang those great religions, Judaism, Christianity, and Mohammedanism. The character of this people is a reflection of the geography of the country they inhabit. Roaming the arid deserts, or concentrating around narrow fertile belts and centres of commerce, they were most deeply impressed with the stern and implacable aspect of Nature. Their belief in their own one God excluded all others, and reacting on their arrogance and self-conceit, made them intolerant and overbearing, and declare all religions but their own unmitigatedly false. The Semetic race has never comprehended civilization, never founded an organic empire, made any discovery in science or mechanical invention, or even produced a work of plastic art. Deficient in power of organization and discipline necessary for military undertakings, its battles have been fought by mercenaries. The Israelitish branch shows less aptitude for political life than the others. It seems to have placed no value on liberty except so far as its religion was concerned, accepting vassalage without a struggle if this was not interfered with. Their wisdom never surpassed parables and proverbs. Even the higher branch, the Arabians, were only able to seize for a brief time the products of Greek thought. Their science was only a miserable translation of the Greek sages; and it has been shown that even these translations were the work of Spaniards and Persians. Pure as are the moral precepts of Jesus, son of Sirach, or Hillel, or the Bible, they are not purer or more exalted than those of Grecian writers. The aphorisms by which the chief relations of morality are expressed are common to all peoples. Of all nations, the Jews should be the last to become the moral standard-bearers. They were hard, narrow, egotistical, arrogant, presuming, superstitious, ignorant, and a type of bigotry. Their dull minds received from their forced contact with Persia all the spiritualism which enlivens the dreary realism of their theology. At Babylon they imbibed the idea of angels and demons, the terrestrial manifestation of Deity, faith in immortality, resurrection of the body, Messianic longings, and belief in the near approach of the end of the world. Dwarfed in everything else, they were characteristically religious, but their religion had no relation to their morality. David, with all his abominable vices, was a man pleasing to the Lord, and no one found fault with him. The Semitic standard was by no means such as Europeans would adopt. In religion, in its strictest interpretation, distinct from morality — the observance of rites and ceremonies, and the bigoted and superstitious opposition to innovation—the Jews are preëminent. They cannot be accused of being excessively moral, but their religion has bound them together and preserved them through the vicissitudes of two thousand years of oppression. Utterly selfish from the beginning, they expressed no sentiment suggestive of the fatherhood of God or brotherhood of man. Jehovah was only a God of the Jews, and gave all other peoples to them to slaughter or enslave if they pleased. They did not wish to extend the sway of their religion. They sought not converts; they rather objected to Gentile dogs professing their faith. Such was the Jewish spirit. It was concreted in a series of books called the Old Testament, pronounced an inspired writing, and really the means whereby its possessors achieved their lofty standing. The claim has been most unfortunate for mankind. The book cannot pretend to teach science, for whenever it attempts to explain natural phenomena it is false. It is not to teach rules of government, for the precepts it presents are in favor of theocracy, slavery, and despotism. If its mission is to teach morals, the national character was none the better for it, the Jews being among the most immoral and turbulent nations of antiquity. A compilation might be made from classic authors which would have a higher moral tone and fewer degrading examples. It is only useful as part of a religious system exclusive and arrogant. Its critical study reveals the fact that the Hebrews were subject to the same law of development as other races. If they received a divine revelation, it did not change the course of evolution. Indelible traces of Fetishism are visible in their latest theology, and Polytheism was for ages entertained. Frequent reference is made to strange gods, whose existence is not denied. Jehovah is not the only god—he is only the most powerful. The claim that he is the One God is of comparatively recent date. The character given him by the Old Testament is contradictory and changeable. He is the Creator and Divine Father, and again only the God of the Jews; almighty and omnipotent, omniscient, eternal and unchanging, and again environed with all the limits of human nature. He walks on the earth, carries on conversation, sleeps, rises early in the morning, is angry, jealous, revengeful, vindictive and avaricious. The advance is easily traced. The family god became that of the nation, and at length the only God. Monotheism was attained in Palestine at nearly the same time it was in Greece. Human sacrifice to this god—most dreadful superstition!—lingered long in the Jewish mind. It is met with in the histories of all nations, and its ultimate form is the foundation of Christianity—the sacrifice of Christ. The offering of Isaac, and of his daughter by Jephthah in fulfillment of a vow—not rashly given, but on a momentous occasion—are not condemned, but rather considered worthy examples of piety, showing beneath a black and fathomless abyss of superstition.

The Aztecs furnish a striking example of this stage of religious thought carried to its fullness. Their vast pyramids were sacrificial mounds. The long line of priests winding up their steep sides, their summits crowned with gory altars where hecatombs of human victims were immolated with all the pageantry imagination could invent; the shrine before which the palpitating hearts were placed by the red hands of the priest who rent them from the bosoms of the struggling victims, all were witnessed by the trembling thousands below, impressed with *reverence* by the dreadful spectacle.

The progress from Fetishism, with its bloody sacrifices and horrid customs, to Monotheism is over an exceedingly long and bloody road, but one which has been traversed by all civilized nations. Religion by this progressive growth becomes a unit differing only in degree in its lowest and highest phases. The Hebrew prophets seem to have first received Monotheism, and to have attempted to raise the people out of Fetishism. The struggle was severe and bloody, the people often relapsing into grossest idolatry. They set up stone pillars, worshiped Ramphan and Chiun, made a golden calf after the bull Apis of the Egyptians, worshiped the serpent, and Baal, Astarte, Thammuz, and Moloch in the pure Fetish spirit, which was deeply impressed on their laws, sacrifices, rites, prohibition of certain food, prescription of garments, and ornaments of the priests.

The struggle between Monotheism and the old Polytheistic faith was remorseless. Extermination of unbelievers is the divine charge. The Infinite Father God rides on the chariots of war and directs the conflict. Even in modern times, when the Moslem extended the sway of Monotheism with the sword, the most horrible cruelty was practiced ; and Christianity, forgetting its suffering founder and the lesson of love he inculcated, has unsheathed its sword and been equally remorseless. This is the dire result of religion. Always claiming infallibility and absolute truth, it knows no mercy, pauses at no inhumanity, stays its hand at no crime.

Fetishism, Polytheism, and Monotheism, are but expressions of one religion, differing only in degree. Standing on the high lands of science, looking down the interminable vista of the past, progress from animal worship and cannibalism to please God, the toil and struggle by which it has been achieved can be comprehended Although its phenomena shall all vanish, its rites and ceremonies—from the repast on human flesh, the quivering heart torn from the breast by the red-handed priest and thrown palpitating before his god, to the sacramental supper of the blood and body of the crucified Jesus—sink like waves in the smooth expanse of ocean ; but the effects these have wrought on human progress shall not perish, for through them we breath the pure air of certain knowledge of the present.

Monotheism is not the goal of this advance. It is only a temporary and incomplete expression of a great theory. It is the last term in a long series of expressions—the last, for beyond, theory yields to fact, empiricism to knowledge. The night of object-worship has vanished before the dawn of the day of thought.

The age of Fetishism is the age of superstition ; both are

products of ignorance and fear, and indivisible. In that brutal epoch when God is everything and man nothing, where the real requirements and objects of life are unknown, the mind prostrate with fear, the wildest fancies of man's relations to God prevail. He is the great chief, the great warrior of the universe. He requires all the petty servility of a tribal tyrant, and is enraged or pleased in a similar manner. Man he created for his own pleasure, and man must bow and be his slave. But he is thrown into darkness; he cannot see the light nor understand what is wanted; he can only be guided by his experience with his petty rules. In regard to the Infinite, he is in a cave, traveling a morass, mistaking the fantastic will-o'-wisps for the beacon-light of God's laws. He is fearful of enjoying himself, for he may thereby incur the wrath of an offended Deity. He stands on some problem for which he fancies a solution, bases his conclusions on such false premises, and wanders world-wide from the truth. Matter and God are in antagonism. Man is a fallen being; he has unpardonably offended the gods; certain sacrifices are demanded as atonement. What a series of dogmas having no foundation in Nature, yet reacting with blasting effect!

God is arbitrary in his demands. The choicest furs of the savage chase, the best part of the slain animal, the finest portion of the scant harvest, the best of the spoils of war are demanded of the devotee, who, so far as God is concerned, or in the recognition of his wishes, might as well be blind. Advancing, God demands greater sacrifices —the best of the flocks and herds, a certain portion of the captives made in war, unusually fine instruments of war, the immolation of members of the tribe or family. The despotic tyrant who rules the universe loves the smoke of reeking altars; his nostrils dilate with the smell of blood; the odor of rare and costly spices is grateful to him. Isaac, the beloved son, is an accepted offering to the bloody Jehovah. Diana, in anger, demands the daughter of Agamem non. The watchful care of Terminus must be repaid by a victim.

God will be aroused to sympathy and pity by cruelty inflicted upon ourselves. Lacerating the flesh with thongs—wearing haircloth until the bones are exposed by its constant chafing; standing on high pillars exposed to the pitiless elements; a living death in a cloister, cell, or dungeon, plunged in the wilderness; denial of the healthy appetites; endurance of hunger, thirst, cold and heat—rejoices the heart of the relentless Deity.

This is the nightmare of religion; nor has the age awakened out of the horrid dream. Ignorance is yet the master, and fear narcotizes mankind. Terrible dream! Hell yawning beneath our feet, devils innumerable with infinite power, and a heartless despot—absolute in his egotism—overriding all!

Mankind have not awoke, except to gaze, as in twilight, between sleeping and waking. Fetishism maintains its hold, and superstition—like ragweeds, rank and foul—occupies the garden of the soul.

The old Satan of Oriental theogony has a supreme place. Hell is still heated with burning sulphur. The Infinite Father is yet a God of battles. Man is a worm created for his iron feet to crush, or to hand over by the million to eternal torment. A priesthood despotically organized keeps the saddle and guides humanity with gag and spur. They demand observance of sacred days, have their sacred books, and prayers which are not to be omitted. God is not pleased that we place our children on altars and thrust the knife into their bosoms. He does not desire our enemy's blood, or the flesh of our flocks, or the first of our harvest, but he demands the sacrifice of our pleasures; he wants us to weep and wail and crucify our spirits. He loves to have us sacrifice the appetites he has given us—the emotions of love and affection. He is pleased to have us cast reason aside for blind and unthinking faith, and re ceive the words of his priests as the ultimate of knowledge without questioning.

The Indian loves tobacco, and he thinks the Great Spirit does also. The choicest bundle of leaves is placed on his altar. The priest hates reason and knowledge; he thinks his God must hate them too, and demands the civilized man to lay his reason on the altar of his conjuration. No; Fetishism has not passed so long as Christian churches in their most sacred communion imitate the cannibal in his worship. He sacrifices the captive seized in war, and afterwards sits down to a horrid repast with his comrades. They meet, and in "lovefeast" break and eat the body and drink the blood of a crucified God!

"Oh!" you say, "it is only as a spiritual type." Do you forget that the great Church of Christianity holds unflinchingly that the words of a priest convert the bread and wine into real flesh and blood?

With the addition of hate, superstition becomes fanaticism. Superstition and bigotry go mad. Becoming firmly persuaded that its dogmas are right, and all others wrong it wages an unconditional war of annihilation. Religion propagates itself by the sword. Mohammedanism has been long cited as its type, but it has drawn the sword no more than Christianity.

Monotheism by its exclusiveness instills this venom into the veins of its believers. Polytheism, although occasionally spasmodically persecuting, knew nothing of this mode of proselytism. Yet this exclusiveness or persecution is not peculiar to Monotheism, only more persistent. The Egyptians were as exclusive as the Jews. It was pollution for them to drink from the same cup with one of another faith. So jealous were they of their gods, that to kill an ibis or a cat was a capital offense, and sufficient to drive a whole city to frenzy. Even the Greeks manifested this spirit inherent in religion. Their laws against Atheism were severe. Many of their philosophers were exiled, and one at least answered with his life. Even the laws written by the philosophers for their imaginary republics were intolerant. They in no instance recognized religious liberty. If the Christian system is right and true, bigotry is blessed; fanaticism, its intensest form, most praiseworthy; and persecution, proceeding to its direst extent, a blessing to the sufferers. For if believing as the Church believes is to save us from the everlasting tortures of hell-fire, does not the priestly inquisitor, who tears and bruises our flesh until our hardness of heart be overcome, and we follow his dictates, confer a favor by bestowing on us the everlasting bliss of heaven ? Goodness and benevolence of heart wedded to ignorance has thus been corrupted, and it has been paradoxically but truly said, the better the ignorant man the more cruel he is as a persecutor.

Christianity is said to be a religion of love, teaching the fatherhood of God and the brotherhood of man, and thereby changing his moral character. The real influence it has exerted may be read in history. Persecuted at first, it grew strong, and turning, it fleshed its fangs in its opponent. Read of the millions of martyrs bound to racks, burned at the stake, torn by red-hot hooks and pincers, starved, lacerated, buried in thick walls of masonry, suffering living deaths in fœtid dungeons. Read the narratives of religious wars—most terrible of wars—of massacres, of autos-da fé. Read of crusades sacrificing nations of warriors for the childish possession of a vacant sepulchre. Worse than all, view a great and gigantic power, having the control of the mental atmosphere of the world, stifling every new thought, every attempt at advancement; claiming science and philosophy as tributaries, and as freely dictating in their realms, as freely employing the thumbscrew and dungeon on their votaries, as on heretics to its own incomprehensible vagaries.

Christianity has assisted human advancement in the same manner that a brake assists the progress of a locomotive·

Its fanaticism forms a page of history unequaled in demoniac cruelty—in foul and malignant venom—in that of any other faith. Professing universal love and peace, it has gone forth like one of the dreadful genii called into being by Arabian fancy—the Bible in one hand, a dripping sword and chains in the other, while from its black lips it has hoarsely shouted, "Believe or be damned !" Men ran wild at the approach of the goblin. Flagellants scattered themselves in armies over Europe ; anchorites perched themselves on towers ; hermits sought caves and mountains by thousands ; the whole world would turn monk or nun.

It was high carnival. The day was darkened by the smoke of charring human flesh—the night illuminated with the blazing fagot. The plains of Europe were continually strewn with the wreck of armies bearing aloft the cross—emblem of the only true religion—engaged in exterminating warfare over unintelligible dogmas.

Deep in dungeons, far from the blushing light of day, the pious inquisitor plied his dreadful trade, and holy priests and worshipful saints stood by and smiled when the tightening screws made the heretic writhe, or a moan to fall from his ashen lips. What were these holy men doing ? They were at the noblest of all possible employment—they were saving souls! They were compelling rebellious and ever simple human nature to walk in the straight and narrow way prescribed in the Bible and their creed. Alas! too well they plied their holy arts. The groans that ascend from the fields of battle are silenced by the cries from the dungeon, scaffold and gibbet, the never-ending wail of despair from the widow and orphan, where the minions of the Spectre have busily worked.

With this black record of crimes ; with hands red with the blood of earth's bravest sons ; with garments purple with clotted gore ; and with a history showing that she has fought to the death every advance of the race, cursed every new discovery in science, attempted to suppress every invention whereby the condition of mankind has been ameliorated ; always siding with tyranny, aristocracy, and slavery—Christianity has the effrontery to raise its voice and claim itself the cause of civilization ! The method it has pursued in advancing knowledge is unique. It was by substituting a blind faith in the place of reason, creeds and dogmas in the place of knowledge, miracle in the place of law. It was by silencing Keplar, burning Giordano Bruno, imprisoning Galileo, opposing its flat earth to the schemes of Columbus, excommunicating the sciences, throwing them out of the schools it carefully controlled. Outside of the Church, despite its influence, with social ostracism and death suspended over them, daring students explored the secrets of Nature ; in seclusion others pursued philosophy ; others in the arena of politics studied national polity. By the concentration of all, the nations were forced onward, dragging this dead weight of creeds and dogmas which now claim to be the cause of the civilization attained. As well might it be claimed for a millstone suspended to the neck of a strong swimmer, because he sustained himself despite its weight, that it sustained him and preserved his life!

At present, the fangs which projected from those gory lips cannot flesh themselves in the heterdox thinker. The talons are dulled and cannot lacerate, but the will remains as strong as ever. This hag, ignorant of Nature, of human nature, and of God—hating opposing beliefs, and trembling with brute fear—is subject to recurrent fits of madness. Within her influence the best emotions of mankind gather mould from the dank and blasting atmosphere. Outside of it, learning has thriven, morality waxed strong ; and Governments, upheld by the potent strength of Justice bestowed by knowledge, chain Superstition and Fanaticism, and compel them to respect human rights.

CHAPTER VI.

VALUE OF THE OLD AND NEW TESTAMENTS AND SACRED BOOKS AS AUTHORITIES.

Hopeful and glorious are the times when men can exercise the right to speak and publish the truth.—TACITUS.

The application of criticism to the Bible in the same manner that it is applied to other literary works is of recent date. The wonderful erudition of German scholars has yielded astonishing results in this field, and exalted criticism itself to the rank of a science. Most English and American theologians dispute their method, and maintain that dogmatic theology is the only means by which truth can be ascertained. They receive the Bible by unthinking and indiscriminating faith.

If the Bible is of human origin, it is subject to the canons of criticism, like other human efforts; if from God, the fact that it was revealed through the human mind and for human understanding makes it at most but a higher degree of human effort, and hence subject to the rules by which all such efforts are to be judged. The assumption and dogmatism of those who would introduce the Bible as supernatural into a natural world are **fast** meeting the disrespect they deserve.

Subjected to this criticism—**judged** by human expedients—what is the result? Historically, the Old Testament is a collection of all the books extant in the Hebrew and Chaldee languages up to a certain period. These were believed to have been written by inspiration, by the Jews and Christians; the apocryphal portion being of later production, and not sacred.

Of the number of books in the Old Testament there is diversity of statement. Josephus makes twenty-two—the number of letters in the Hebrew alphabet ; others make twenty-seven ; the Talmud is not certain of twenty-four ; the number now retained is thirty-nine. In different manuscripts the order in which they are placed varies, although their general arrangement is very old. The Apocrypha was at first only an addition to the Alexandrian version, and was first regarded as a whole by the Protestant. Luther arranged the books in a manner to please himself.

The Bible is interesting as being one of the earliest written books, and hence preserving the oldest forms of thought.

Who were its authors ? Moses is said to have written the Laws ; and it is certain that there was no literature before the school of Samuel. Critical acumen has determined that the four books referred to Moses, and perhaps Joshua, were written in the age of Solomon ; Judges and Samuel still later ; and not until the eighth century before Christ were the oracles of the Prophets inscribed. After the exile, Ezra and Nehemiah wrote new books of their own, and perhaps glossed those already extant. The Pentateuch was completed about the time of Josiah ; the prophetic portion some time after Nehemiah ; the heterogeneous Hagiographia was slowly accumulated as new Psalms were written and new prophets prophesied, and about the close of the Persian period became permanently arranged. Well knowing the story of the miraculous resstoration of the corrupted text to be a fable, theologians adhere to it for want of a more plausible explanation. That the priests preserved the national record is probable from their known office in other nations, and the character of the books themselves. Thus preserved, they slowly accumulated during ages not characterized by activity of thought. The most ancient mention of the Old Testament collection was made 130 B. C., by Jesus, son of Sirach, but he does not declare it complete. Josephus enumerates twenty-two books, and places its conclusion in the time of Artaxerxes Longimanus. As the Jews regarded themselves as a sacred nation, everything pertaining to them, even their records, were sacred (Ex. xix., 6), and they regarded all their writers as divinely inspired. This was their earliest belief; but later, with the greater activity of thought, they began to have doubts, and were conscious of the departure of inspiration. They had no means of drawing the line between the inspired and uninspired writings. Malachi, as the last of the Prophets, closed the glorious era of inspiration, according to the current belief, yet Jesus, son of Sirach, deserves the title of Prophet far more than many of those who are canonized. With the first Temple the spirit of inspiration departed, according to the Talmudists.

The present Old Testament was by no means the only collection; there were others equally venerated by their possessors. The Samaritans received only the writings of Moses, whom they regarded as the only great and true religious teacher directly inspired. The Alexandrian canon rejected the apocryphal books, adding them as an appendix. To obtain a clear idea of the text preserved, the books rejected and lost must be considered. Mention is made in the preserved sacred writings of other books equally valuable of which not a vestige remains. These are the Book of the Wars of Jehovah, Book of Jasher, Book of the Constitution of the Kingdom, Solomon's Three Thousand Proverbs, Solomon's Three Thousand and Five Songs, Solomon's Works on Natural History, Book of the Acts of Solomon, Book of the Chronicles of the Kings of Israel and of Judah, Chronicles of King David, Books of Samuel the Seer, of Nathan, of Gad the Seer, Prophecy of Abijah, Book of Shemaiah, Book of Jehu, History of the

Book of Josiah, Sayings of Hosea, and a Second book of
Lamentations. These represent a mass of revelation equal,
if not superior, to that which has been preserved. The
most fortuitous circumstances determined the loss or preservation of these books—the whim of a priest; the accidents
of war; the caprice of the possessor to change, mutilate, or
destroy. Knowing this, well may it be asked how it is
possible to be guided by a revelation one half of which is
lost. Nor are we assured the lengthy list of titles of books
irrecoverably lost embraces a tithe of those books which
have not even left a recorded name. Yet this collection
was received in its various versions by Jesus and his followers as sacred and authoritative. The New Testament
writers do not appear to have had the least idea that they
were writing sacred books. They gave plain narratives of
events, or simply letters to the churches, which were
slowly gathered into the collection known as the New Testament. Apostolic fathers rarely cite the apostolic writings, only three vague allusions being made to them, and
their mention of the Evangelists is equally uncertain.
They allude to the Apochryphal Gospels in the same
manner as to the genuine. In the time of Justin Martyr,
who died one hundred and sixty-six years after Christ, the
Gospels were not regarded as sacred writings. He mentions them as "The Memories of the Apostles," and
receives books now lost and rejects many now regarded as
holy. Scarcely ten years later, Dionysius, Bishop of Cor-
inth, refers to them as "The Scriptures of our Lord,"
showing the slow growth of the belief in the sacredness of
the miscellaneous writings, and preparing the way for their
collection. The first alluded to was in the possession of
Marcion, and consisted of the Pauline Epistles and the
Gospel of Luke. It was made in Pontus, and brought to
Italy under the title of the "Gospel," or the "Apostle."
About the beginning of the third century the extension of
Christianity brought forward all the writings relating to

the subject from their ignoble obscurity, and the principal teachers quoted them as authorities. While the three great leaders, Irenæus, Tertullian, and Clement of Alexandria, agreed in receiving the four Gospels, the Acts, thirteen Pauline Epistles, First Epistles of Peter and of John, and the Apocalypse; the first received the Second of John ; the second, the Epistle of Philemon and of Jude; the third, Hebrews, and quotes apocryphal Gospels—as that of the Egyptians—in the same manner as he did the true. The idea of the sacredness of the writings had gained strong hold, and Irenæus speaks of the "Divine Scriptures," and as being "perfect, since they are dictated by the Logos of God and his Spirit." He, in unison with Tertullian and Clement, thought the Holy Spirit dictated the words to the writers, and founded this claim on the internal evidence of the writings, the character of the writers, and tradition. They were satisfied with this test ; but its worthlessness is made apparent by their not agreeing among themselves on the position of many of these books—a failure more clearly manifested by an examination of the early Fathers. Who should be a better Judge than Origen? yet he rejected Hebrews, James, the Second Epistle of Peter, the Second and third of John, and Jude, receiving as inspired the Shepherd of Hermas and the Epistle of Barnabas. Eusebius regarded the Epistles of James and Jude, the Second of Peter, the Second and Third of John, as disputed; and as spurious, the Acts of Paul, the Shepherd, the Apocalypse of Peter, and the Institutes of the Twelve Apostles. The Apocalypse of John and Hebrews were regarded as genuine by some and spurious by others. It would be interesting to know on what evidence the judgment rested.

Outside of the spurious works, further removed from the genuine, were a host of others forged by heretics to support peculiar doctrines, and so plainly indicating their origin as to cause no discussion. Cyril (three hundred and forty-eight years after Christ) endorsed fourteen Epistles of Paul, and Athanasius accepted the Wisdom of Solomon, the Wisdom of Sirach, Esther, Judith, Tobit, the Doctrines of the Apostles, and the Shepherds.

The decisions of the Councils winnowed the vast accumulation of writings. The assembled priests assumed the right of condemnation, and exercised it most unsparingly. Those writings only were accepted as divine which expressed the views of the majority of the Council; but as the Councils were composed of different members whose opinions varied, the decisions of one often reversed those of the others, and books now regarded as of vital importance, for centuries oscillated between canonical and apocryphal.

Having learned by this brief outline the origin of the Bible, the wholly human means of its inception, we ask if the transmission of this holy compilation has been through pure and uncontaminating channels. If the Scriptures are inspired, and contain knowledge man in no other manner can acquire, their value entirely depends on their absolute purity. It is not only essential that they be revealed, but also transmitted uncontaminated.

The Hebrew, in which the greater portion of the Old Testament is written, is the the oldest or first developed of the Semitic languages, and its decline had set in when the later prophets wrote. After the exile it ceased to be spoken, and was familiar only to the learned, becoming virtually a dead language. Here is the cause of the veneration for the old books. They were written in a language understood only by the priests, who thus became necessary to interpret their hidden meaning to the people. Those who have studied modern languages of the same family as their own, and have attempted to perfectly translate ideas from one to the other, will appreciate the task of translating this oldest of written tongues. The spirit of the words has wings, and no power can retain it. The difficulty here is augmented by the scantiness of explanatory materials. The Rabbins were not agreed two thousand years ago on the meaning of important passages, yet their traditions are relied on by one school as of great importance, while held in contempt by another.

The old versions have been employed to gain a meaning of the original Hebrew, as well as the Alexandrian, Syriac, Arabic of Rabbi Saadia, Gaou, Vulgate, and Chaldee paraphrases. Not understanding the original Hebrew, the expounder would learn how to correctly translate from the translations made into Greek, Arabic, Syriac, Chaldee, and Latin. If these earlier translators were not inspired equally with the original penman, what surety is there of their freedom from error, or that they express the word of God?

The Alexandrian version, or Septuagint, is of unknown origin, Eichhorn and others having incontestably proved the story of the seventy-two learned Jews producing it at the instance of Demetrius Phalereus a fable. It was not only used by the Greeks, but by the Jews themselves, until in combats with the Christians they were compelled to retreat to the original Hebrew, and finding the version incorrect, began to detest it.

Aquila, in the beginning of the second century, made a literal translation into Greek, which the Jews preferred to the Septuagint. Some of the early Fathers accuse him of falsifying to overthrow the testimony respecting Christ, but others quote him without remark when his text applies to their doctrines better than the Septuagint. The dissatisfaction with the latter version appears from the numerous others constantly being made, for even then the greatest difficulty was experienced in obtaining the real significance of the Hebrew words and phrases. Origen attempted to show the errors by publishing various esteemed versions in parallel columns, to find his labor result in a most fearful corruption of the text. Careless and designing copyists misplaced the names of the versions, omitted or misplaced the critical marks, and passages from other Greek versions, written in the margin, were copied into the body of the work.

This corrupt text reacted on the Septuagint, revisions of which were made with a liberal hand by successive copyists, until it became almost equally corrupt. Lucian and Hesychius, three hundred and eleven years after Christ, wrote a corrected copy, which was considered as the best authority by Jerome, from whom we learn that among the various churches the different editions of the Septuagint were in use. He wrote: "The common edition is different in different places the world over. . It is corrupted everywhere to meet the views of the place and time, or the caprice of the transcribers."

Of the Latin versions from the Greek text, Augustine says they cannot be counted. These had become more corrupt than the Greek. Jerome says: "For the most part, among the Latins there are as many different Bibles as copies of the Bible; for every man has added or subtracted according to his own caprice, as he saw fit." He was so disgusted with this sacrilegious transcription that he undertook a Latin version direct from the Hebrew. It met with great opposition at first, but came into general use, and shared the fate of its predecessors in becoming corrupted by the carelessness or design of transcribers. .

How easily this was accomplished cannot be comprehended in this age of printed books, when a thousand or ten thousand copies are printed exactly alike. As all the various translations were used, students would write on the margins of their copies corresponding passages and extracts from other versions, and erase and correct when they thought errors had been made. In transcribing, the zealous believer interpolated or blended passages, omitted or inserted words, often to explain or to adapt the passage to singing. Even pillars of the Church, in order to sustain their dogmas, erased or inserted passages to uphold their doctrines. Those who re-transcribed often placed the marginal notes in the body of the work, or re-corrected from other manuscripts they believed more correct.

The Vulgate having thus become exceedingly corrupt, in 802 Charlemagne appointed Alcuin to correct it, and ordered the reception of his copy.

In the eleventh century, Lanfranc, Archbishop of Canterbury, undertook a new revision; and in the twelfth, Cardinal Nicolaus applied himself to the never-accomplished task. Bacon repeatedly testifies to the failure to improve the corrupted text. The translators and expounders were all human.

With the discovery of printing and the unprecedented multiplication of copies, the necessity of a correct text became of utmost consequence. The Council of Trent at once silenced, in a manner peculiar to infallible power, all discussion by declaring that the Vulgate should be held authentic—the Church furnishing the text—and all private editions should have no authority. At that time, in this same Church-established text, Isidore Clarius pointed out eighty thousand errors. To crown this most stupendous imposition, the Pope, as infallible head of the Church, undertook to furnish the authentic edition both of the Old and New Testaments, which were published as infallible, and to add to or extract from which was pronounced a crime.

After this brief review, in the light of history, what is the evidence of the genuineness of the Bible? The Old Testament was written we know not when or by whom. It is the fragments of literature of an insignificant people, written in a dead language, the key to which is lost. Its translation two thousand years ago was extremely difficult. The New Testament was written at the close of the first and during the second century. Its authors are unknown. Its compilation was accomplished by a most singular method. The divine character of its books was determined by human reason, which rejected and destroyed all those books in any way opposed to the orthodox faith. Thus obtained, the text was corrupted by ignorance, carelessness or design, until — whether Latin, Greek, or Hebrew — it became concealed beneath the accumulated rubbish. From this source the modern translations were made.

Protestantism has worked its way back to the Jewish canon and the Greek, thus illuminating, as it asserts, the errors of translation and transcription; but this is more apparent than real, as the text was corrupted in the original beyond all critical power to renovate. This Catholicism acknowledged, and by a decision of one of its Councils (Trent) declared the Latin Vulgate the absolute Scriptures which if any one despise, "let him be accursed." The Catholic bows in acquiescence to the Council; the Protestant points scornfully to the proven fallibility of the Councils, and is assured they have no right to issue such a decree. Yet this decree of the majority in Council is the basis on which the New Testament rests its claims to inspiration.

First there were miscellaneous writings read for instruction, but not considered divine. After a century or more they began to be in great esteem and to be slowly collected, the dominant sect holding to those which best agreed with its doctrine, and rejecting the others as spurious. This process continued until a compilation was effected, and the party receiving it had power to decree the collection the only true and inspired writings. Who dare deny that the reception or rejection of one and all of these books, now considered as divine authority, did not rest on human judgment? Is it possible that a direct revelation from God would be subject to such test or accompanied with such obscurity? If God *should* make a revelation, it would come indisputable as the sun of morning, and no holy father, pious priest, or bigoted Council be called on to decide which portions should be retained or rejected. This conclusion follows as a logical necessity. If the early Fathers or the Catholic Councils had power to determine the true from the erroneous, every man now has the same power and the granted right to revoke the decisions of all his predecessors. History reveals the human origin of the books themselves, and exposes the superstition and arrogance of those who collected them, and compelled the acknowledgment of the divine character of their work. They were simply men, often ignorant, always prejudiced by their religion, and the only right they had to sit in judgment was their own conceited bigotry. The whole world is open to every human soul, and none have the right to foreclose their opportunity.

CHAPTER VII.

MAN'S MORAL PROGRESS DEPENDENT ON HIS INTELLECTUAL GROWTH.

If the Jews had not made a beginning, some other nation would have offered the requisite organs, and those organs would have guided the advance in precisely the same manner, only transferring to some books, now probably lost, the sacred character which is still attributed to others.—COMTE.

ALL civilized races of men have books which they regard as sacred, and to which they refer their knowledge of moral law and the foundation of religion. Such books are accepted as direct revelations from their God. They all—Vedas, Shaster, Koran, Testament (Old and New)—make one claim of divine origin, its consequent infallibility, and that they are absolutely essential for man's understanding of the will of his Maker.

As the Bible is more intimately related to us, and as we regard no other volume as sacred, it may be regarded as a type of all others. We shall reach the conclusion, if we investigate this realm over which superstition has spread for immemorial time her forbidding pinions, that mankind have derived little benefit from their moral codes except as they have comprehended them by their intellect. Man's moral progress has been and is equivalent to intellectual growth. Until moral truths become the property of the intellect they remain barren beliefs, or united with superstition are productive of great evil.

In the vast volume of universal history not one page can be pointed out wherein Christianity contributed to social or intellectual advancement. On the contrary, it has invariably arrayed itself with the Old, and by every possible means sought to retard humanity's growth. This is its necessary position; it is a part of the Old, and must battle for it. Claiming the infallibility conferred by direct inspiration, it cannot retract. Its creed renders growth impossible. A perfect God writes word by word a perfect infallible revelation for infinite time and generations. Such a revelation cannot expand—it is complete and finished. To add thereto is to blemish. Thus presented, the Church divides on the method of its interpretation. The Protestant gives to each man the right to interpret for himself. In this it is most illogical; for how is a finite, imperfect, fallible being to interpret and comprehend an infinite, infallible revelation? When the right of reason is granted, the finite and fallible status of the Bible is acknowledged. The right to reason presupposes the right to receive or reject; for of what use is reason unless this right is granted? Protestantism founders in this absurdity. Really occupying the identical grounds of Catholicism, it grants the right to reason, but refuses the right of rejection; it says: "Believe, or be damned." Reason may exercise itself on the Bible, but in such a manner as to receive it. If infallible, reason is needless—if infinite, it is impossible. Protestantism denies both these qualities when it assumes the right of private judgment and breaks the path for radical Infidelity. If Luther, Calvin, or Melancthon has the right to protest against Rome, Beecher, Murray, or Parker may protest against them, and the end is a universal individual protest, there being as many sects as persons, and thorough and complete individualization.

Catholicism maintains the severest logic. It stifles reason at the beginning. It truly says finite man cannot comprehend an infinite revelation; hence God has chosen teachers to interpret his revelation; the priesthood is as necessary as the Bible itself; to ordinary men it is a book written in a foreign tongue, and the inspired priest only can translate and apply it to mortal wants.

How far has the intellectual life of the race been benefitted by the Bible? It cannot claim scientific accuracy or knowledge, for it accepts the views of Nature received by the rude and savage Semitic people. They believed the world to be a perfectly square and flat island floating on the water beneath the firmament. It was stationary, and the sun, moon, and stars revolved around it. This is the accepted theory of the Bible, and so understood by its believers, and scarcely three centuries have passed since the man would have been burned who dared to assert otherwise. Its cosmogony is that of conjecturing ignorance. Did not *God* know that his world was a ball, and the sun—not the earth—was the central body? Knowing these facts, he writes the very reverse in his revelation, leaving those whom he seeks to enlighten by his revelation to discover the truth by painful research.

It is urged that this is a wrong view of the intentions of the Deity. He adapted his words to the comprehension of the savage Hebrew. He would not have been understood had he spoken in the phrase of modern science. He adapted his words to their comprehension. This revelation, then, becomes a special affair for the exclusive benefit of a small tribe, and cannot be urged on the present; for if intended for infinite generations it must have infinite extension and application.

It is interesting to trace the progress of ideas and the slow yielding of the interpretation of the Bible. From the dawn of Science to the present a constant battle has been waged. Every new truth is fought to the death, and after the Church finds it cannot withstand it, it turns and claims it for its own. Geology dealt the death-blow to the Mosaic cosmogony. The earth created in six days? Turn over the leaves of the grest rock-volume, stratum reposing upon stratum for fifteen miles of crust, replete with vestiges of organic beings, once swimming, flying, creeping, or walking, successively evolved while millions of millions of ages rolled away. A billion years is but a single swing of the pendulum which marks the progressive evolution of worlds. Geology and Genesis can never be reconciled. The story is not an allegory, but an attempt of the ignorant savage mind to account for phenomena it did not comprehend. It is the same with all its pretended explanations, as witness that of the rainbow. It is not the sunbeam painting itself on the descending drops of the shower, but a sign set by God after the Flood for the comfort and assurance of Noah, and for a thousand years this interpretation prevailed. Now we know that a thousand of ages before Noah's time, on the wild and desolate shores of the new red sandstone the winds blew the raindrops, and can we suppose that when those dark showers rolled away, and the low sun shone on their pearly drops, no rainbow gorgeously decorated their dark garments?

After the great battle waged on the intellectual field, it is again urged that it is not to teach science, not for intellectual progress, but as a revelation of morals, the Bible was given to man. It was taken as a standard for the intellect as long as the claim could be maintained, and only by compulsion did it relinquish its blighting grasp. Is there better foundation for its claims as the sole teacher of moral truth? Does it teach any truths man would not have arrived at without its aid? It is claimed that it does, and the same claims are made for all sacred books. Against this assertion, so arrogantly maintained, a volume of extracts, wise sayings, and proverbs might easily be compiled from classic writers and the records of remote and even barbarous peoples, which would be in every respect equal or superior to the Bible. What is there in the famous Sermon on the Mount not well known before the first century? Confucius, more than five hundred years previously, taught a code equally pure. The vaunted Golden Rule was expressed by the Chinese sage, and about the same time by Pythagoras in Greece. Were not the ancients moral? Witness their laws and customs. Do they not present lives favorably comparable with the most shining examples of Christian virtue? Plato and Socrates were equal in forgiveness of enemies, in patient endurance of suffering, in all the virtues bestowed by religion on any Christian saint.

But it is said, although the ancient sages wrote wisely and spoke truthfully, though their lives put to blush those of a vast majority of Christians, they could not agree respecting the foundation of virtue, the ultimate object towards which it should be directed, or in what man's happiness consisted. This is a singular objection from the Christian world, who never could agree, with all the light of their revelation, on these same questions, who from the apostles' time have disputed with word and sword, and are now divided into more than a thousand contending sects.

Nothing is more obvious than the independence of ethics of revelation. Revelation is only its accidental expression. This is proven by the fact that all moral truths expressed in the Bible were clearly recognized for indefinite time before its presentation. It abounds in precepts good of themselves, though not original with it, but as a moral code it is exceedingly imperfect. So far from pointing man to the eternally true and right, in the hands of its interpreters it has taught the opposite of truth and blinded those who would see. It advocates slavery. The chosen men of God are slaveholders. He urges them to battle, assists them to gain the day, and directs them how to divide the spoil of captive wives, mothers, and maidens. If in the terrible ordeal of slavery through which we have passed, the slaveholder found consolation anywhere, it was in the Bible. He fought under the direct command of God, who cursed Ham, and his posterity, and declared it just that they should be bondsmen and bondswomen for all time. So directly did the Bible oppose anti-slavery that its only agitators threw it down and trampled it in the dust.

It upholds capital punishment. Its code is a code of vengeance, and although the great thinkers of the day, one and all, oppose the death penalty, and the refined sense of the age revolts at it as a relic of barbarism, the prejudice created and sustained by religious education founded on the Bible preserves it as a black and dismal blot on our civilization. It holds woman in her present unequal position with man, and sets itself directly in the way of her advancement. One of the most startling miracles recorded in the Old Testament is the standing still of the sun and moon to enable the Israelites, pushed on by God, to slaughter their enemies. A religion of peace ? The millions that have perished in its wars are a minority of those who have fallen victims to the stake, the gibbet, and nameless instruments of torture, or suffered a thousand deaths in reeking dungeons, with iron links festering their flesh, without appeal and without hope. The Church has arrogated to itself the authority to do for the living as it believes their God does for nine-tenths of the dead—created a hell, and carried out his commands by commencing those tortures which he will intensify and continue forever.

For the Bible, it is claimed that the human mind could not unaided have arrived at its moral code. Surely the mind of man could not have obtained a just conception of the angry, jealous Jehovah, whose garments were dyed red with the blood of the slain; his creation of the world in six days and then resting; his creation of life and light before he created the sun; his creating man perfect, and man's becoming a most pitiably imperfect work; his drowning all the world except eight souls, who became worse than those destroyed; his self-sacrifice on the cross as the only means of reclaiming a moiety of mankind from the innate and all-powerful principle of evil. This only can be learned by such a revelation. After its acquisition, it requires thousands of years to rid mankind of its incubus. At this stage of the discussion we ask, *can* a book bring new moral truth to man? Can he be taught that which is not inherent in his constituton? The horse cannot comprehend mathematics because the mental qualities necessary are dormant or absent, nor can it understand moral relations for the same reason. The same is true of man. Unless he has the moral qualities, moral truths would fall as unappreciated before him as the animal. He must first possess these moral qualities in order to receive a revelation, and possessing them, they evolve moral truths, and a revelation is not required.

Do not understand that I cast reproach on the Bible. I place it with the sacred books of other races—the Avesta, the Shaster, the Vedas, the Koran—and consider them all as equally creditable records of the strivings and spiritual experiences of childish and savage men to fathom and comprehend the mysteries of the spiritual universe within and the illimitable universe without. One has no more right to command belief than another. Truths are beautifully expressed by all, but no new ones are revealed. They repeat what is inherent in the constitution of man. If all sacred books were blotted from the world this day, not a single truth would be lost. The reception of or acquiescence in an ethical system, in order to work a lasting benefit, must not be by belief, but by knowledge. The system must meet an intellectual development competent to understand and make it its own. It is asserted that the simple belief has power to elevate. Most mischievously false is the assertion. Belief is a dead dogma, and if the believer advances, it is not from the power of his belief, but by intellectual progress. This is demonstrated by the results of missionary labors. Glowing narrations are published of conversions of the natives of the farthest islands of the sea, and the glorious results wrought by the Bible amongst the savages of the frozen north or the burning equator. The zealous missionaries appear to think baptism of the natives indicative of their reception of Christianity. "Blessed book!" say they, "wherever thou goest, civilization and innumerable blessings follow." Oh, missionary! it is not with the Bible that civilization goeth forth, but with the self-reliant Anglo-Saxon. Are savage men changed to Christians? Nay; they vanish like frost before the sun of intelligence. It is not conversion, but the terrible, inevitable law of extinction which is brought into operation. The Red Indian, from a race holding a vast continent, has become a remnant fast expiring—not driven westward, as is poetically said, but *dying* out, as the wolf and deer, on the place of their birth.

The *Missionary Herald* says that "only seven per cent of the population of Ceylon (2,000,000) should profess Christianity, and that only two per cent should be Protestant Christians, will be melancholy facts pregnant with solemn reflections to many of our readers."

Again: "If ours is the day of small things, what can we say to India with her 200,000,000 against our 2,000,000 and her less than half a million Christians, say one fourth of one per cent, against our seven per cent."

"The account Mr. Munger (missionary) gives of the present state and prospects of the Mahratta mission is *not encouraging*. Less than a dozen persons constitute his Sabbath audience, and these are from his own family, and the Christian household connected with the mission."

Of the Chinese missions the *Herald* says, "The pig-tail celestials of the flowery kingdom do not take very kindly to Christianity. With twenty-four missionaries and fifteen native helpers in China, the American Foreign Mission organization reports the baptism of the first convert."

The *Daily Witness*, Montreal, 1866, says: "There are now

twenty-five Protestant missionary societies laboring in India. These societies maintain about five hundred and fifty missionaries, and expend annually in that country not far from $1,550,000."

The Spaniards converted the swarming population of Mexico and Peru; where now are their converts? A charming story, highly suggestive, is related of an Aztec tribe. They were readily persuaded to demolish their idols and set up the cross in their places, and Cortez left them, fully persuaded that they were true believers. It so happened that one of his horses was disabled and left with them. Alas for the worship of the true God! The superstitious natives, connecting the unknown animal with the power of the white man, worshiped it as a deity, gave it flowers and savory viands; and when it pined and died on such inappropriate diet, its afflicted worshipers reared its effigy in stone, and a century later, when the Franciscans came to preach the Gospel, they were astonished to find this image of a horse occuping the highest place in the temple, and devoutly adored as the god of thunder and lightning. The native mind found its level in worship, despite the efforts of the conqueror to force the mystification of the Trinity on the untutored intellect. Were the Aztecs converted? They are gone, and not one remains to read the hieroglyphic tablets of their ancestors. Is the Bible more deadly than the rifle?

One of the most active and zealous missionaries on the African coast confessed that he never converted a single African. Once he thought he had succeeded, but his new convert, on being informed that he must deny himself a plurality of wives, at once denied his religion. Dr. Livingstone says that forty missionaries were sacrificed to the deadly climate of Africa before a single convert was made. After the vast outlay of missionary labor, there is not an important Christian community of their founding constructed of heathen elements. The churches of China and Japan are founded on sand, and despite the intellectual culture and resources of the Jesuits, crumbled. The battle between Christianity and the great Asiatic religions—Buddhism, Brahminism, and Islamism—has not been more fortunate. Islamism has gained the ascendency in Africa, and is fast conquering that continent.

Mr. Hutchins gives the results of ten years' attendance at a mission school on the west coast of Africa in the answer of his servant when asked what he knew of God: "God be very good; he made two things—one, sleep; and the other, Sunday, when no one has to work." He says that after scores of years of intercourse with European traders and missionaries, the Africans still cling "to their gis-gis, jujus, and Fetishism with as much pertinacity as they did many hundred years ago. . . . Here we have all the appliances of our arts, our sciences, and our Christianity, doing no more good than did the wheat in the parable, that was sown among briers and thorns. To attempt civilizing such a race before they are humanized appears to me beginning at the wrong end." Hamilton Smith remarks, "Even Christianity of more than three centuries' duration in Congo has scarcely excited a progressive civilization." No people have more direct communication with Europe than the Africans, amongst whom Christian bishops achieved renown in the times of the primitive fathers, and in modern times numerous missionary stations have been maintained at great sacrifice of money and of life, yet no visible effect has been produced towards civilizing the black race. The people of the torrid zone find in the picturesque and passional teachings of Moslemism greater satisfaction than in the colder and more intellectual forms of Christianity. Where Christianity is apparently received, it proves in the end only a form, and its transcendent doctrines are changed into crudest Paganism. Humboldt saw in the Cordilleras a savage crowd dancing and brandishing their war-hatchets around an altar where a monk was elevating the Host. They simply transferred their war dance around a fire to an altar. Savary states that no Indian has ever become a true Christian. Mr. Kennon, in one of his popular lectures on Northeastern Asia, said the missionaries found it impossible to convey any idea of God or of the atonement to the Yakuts, because their language had no words for any of the high moral conceptions of Europeans. The want of such words indicates the want of the ideas they express—a deficiency supplied only by ages of growth. The Greek priest hangs a cross on the neck of the low-browed, skin-clad Yakut, and reports to St. Petersburg another remarkable conversion to Christianity. The Pagan rites and frantic ceremonies of the Egyptians are now enacted before the churches of the Copts, as described by Herodotus, earliest of historians.

The Greeks still preserve their "Phyrric" dance; the celebrated chorographic dance of the ancient Romans is yet preserved by the Wallachian peasantry, showing how much stronger are customs wrought by indigenous religious faiths than foreign systems, even if they be apparently successful. Wm. H. Seward, in his "Travels Around the World," p. 456, agrees with this universal testimony of unprejudiced observers. His opinion has vastly more weight than those of ordinary travelers, for he possessed superior advantages, and he certainly will not be accused of granting more than it was impossible to avoid against the benefits of missionary labor. "It was not for St. Xavier nor the Catholic Church of the 16th century to bring India and the East into Christian civilization. It must be sadly admitted that this remains yet to be done. It is to be hoped that the great work has been begun in the humble schools for the native men and women which have been opened under missionary auspices in various parts of the country." This is virtually yielding the whole question. It is not religion taught by the missionary, it is knowledge taught in the schools which is expected to elevate Hindoo civilization.

Who can dissent from Renan, when he says: "As to the savage races, those sad survivors of an infant world, for whom nothing better can be wished than a quiet death, it is almost derision to apply our dogmatic formulas to them. Before making Christians of them, we should first have to make them men, and it is doubtful if we should succeed in doing that. The poor Otaheitan is trained to attend mass or sermon, but the incurable softness of his brain is not remedied: he is only made to die of melancholy or *ennui*. Oh! leave these children of nature to fade away on their mother's bosom. Let us not with our stern dogmas, the fruit of twenty centuries of reflection, disturb their childish play, their dances by moonlight, their hour of sweet intoxication." The mistake of devotees is in the belief that morals or religion can be manufactured and forced on the mind. They create their formulas, which they call religion, and regard the observation of these as conversion. This process may be very well here where educational prejudice is in their favor, when they cannot depart very far from the generally received ideas, but when they attempt by such means to storm the religion of other races, they without exception utterly fail. True conversion to our transcendental morality is as possible as the domestication of the tiger or lion; they cannot comprehend our lofty Idealism. This is a question of anatomy and physiology. Its solution depends on the structure and resulting functions of the brain. When the savage is able to grasp the sciences with the acumen of the European, then and not till then can he be truly converted to the European's religion. His thoughts, desires, emotions, character, are what his organization compels; consequently his organization must be changed before any change of character can be expected. Christianity, born from the *débris* of immemorial ages, has grown with the growth of the people who accept it, and is the representative of their theological ideas. Now go to the wilds, and, meeting a savage trained in another school in all respects different, thrust this system upon his attention. He is utterly incapable of its comprehension. There is a wide interval between the savage and the philosopher. We have passed over by slow and painful progress through millions of ages. The savage may receive aid from our acquirements, but we cannot bridge the interval, nor construct a shorter road for his progress.

Religion is organically opposed to progress. The formulas of religion must of necessity be sacred and inviolable; they cannot yield, and soon are left behind. Then commences the great struggle, not to cease until the reign of perfect knowledge. On one side will be constant effort to extend the domain of knowledge—on the other, persecution; for with the belief in infallibility comes the right of enforcing that belief, and faith and bigotry always are in exact ratio to ignorance. There is no limit to the illustrations history furnishes of this subject. Faith in a religion not understood always results in bigotry, superstition, intolerance, and persecution. It might as well be said that a man's coat influenced his mind as that he is organically changed by an exotic system of religion. A church member, a bigot, a fanatic are easily made, but an organically good and upright man is good and upright from development, and cannot be made to order.

In Robespierre and Condorcet, history has furnished examples of the conduct of life of a man biased in early life by his religious instruction, and of the self-sustaining manhood, developed by intellectual and moral culture The picture is drawn in strongest colors, and the nobility in life, and philosophical calmness at the approach of death manifested by the latter, are presented in strong contrast with the pitiless cruelty in life, and shrinking from death of the former.

Robespierre was educated a *protégé* of the Church, and

was deeply imbued with the dogmas of religion. A scholar of the Jesuits, his morality was such as the Church bestows. That he was not an inquisitor was determined by his circumstances. He pledged himself to certain political distractions, and in their defense and extension, as remorselessly shed the blood of hecatombs of victims as the priest sacrifices to convictions.

By nature of tender feeling; resigning his office on being compelled to pass sentence of death; trembling even at the sight of blood, he became the most loathsome monster on whom the light of day ever shone. Having inflamed the populace, until, in obedience to his will, they sacrificed on the guillotine, amid shouts of joy, their king, their queen, their nobility, and decimated even the ranks of the people, he with priestly audacity pronounced an oration on the value of morality, religion, and a belief in a Supreme Being, and organized a festival to the latter, in which he officiated as high priest. The most sacred and holy of all missions to him was a revival of the religious sentiment of the French people. Only two days after this extraordinary display of folly, he prepared to change the revolutionary tribunal, so that he might be able to destroy his opponents, not by the slow process of single condemnation, but by scores and hundreds, thus wielding absolutely a dictatorship of the scaffold. By this last terrible engine he himself was crushed, and when his head fell beneath the same axe to which he had so remorselessly consigned such multitudes of true and noble men and women, in allusion to the worship of the Supreme, of which he would be high priest, a spectator said, "Yes, Robespierre, there is a God!"

Condorcet, cast on these same troublous times, made no pretense to religion. His intellect was keen and cultivated. Thrown into a dungeon, and hourly awaiting the execution, he called for a pen, thinking to leave a defense. "A defense of his personal actions and opinions!

Should he, when so little time was spared, waste it in such idle manner?" No, he reproved himself, and casting aside such vanities, he sat down amid the roar of conflicting factions; the din of revolution already saturated with blood; in his cell, hearing the wails of ten thousand broken hearts, and the famishing cries of a whole nation, and with a sublime faith sought to prove human progress and the ultimate perfectibility of man! With far-reaching sight he looked beyond the petty accidents of his time, to the magnificent result of future ages. He reposed perfect trust in the wisdom of the order of nature, and in life or death submitted himself to her hands. Seeing in himself only an atom of the immeasurable whole; one individual in a countless swarm, he would not thrust forward his personality, but would employ his last short hour in presenting a great principle, which he hoped would prove beneficial to the coming time.

Thus what passes under the name of religious instruction is narrow and selfish to the last degree. It has of itself no broad and expanding principles, and if the devotee becomes ennobled and enlarged, the power either comes from himself or some other source. By aiming one fatal blow at reason, it would transform the man into a blind slave, quaking with servile fear of the gory hag Superstition, and a ready tool of bigotry.

Religious instruction is characterized by this singular quality, the more one is instructed the less one knows. Intellectual and moral culture are alone able to elevate the soul to the grand highlands of philosophy where, wholly above the accidents of the hour, it calmly contemplates the eternal relations of things.

Infinitely better than this puling cant and unmanly sneaking from obligations taken and faults committed, the stoicism of pagan Rome, an Horatius offering himself for his country, a Regulus returning to torture because he had pledged his word, a magnanimity which sank self entirely out of sight, as in the consul Lucius Æmilius, who desperately wounded, after the battle of Cannæ, cried, "Waste not your commiseration on me, but fly to Rome, and garrison her walls. . Let me die in the midst of my slaghtered soldiers!"

It is claimed by the leaders of Christianity that to it we owe our civilization—without it we should still roam the forests of Europe, skin-clad savages, without the least conception of right or wrong. To the general views expressed in the preceding pages we specialize to show the real influence Christianity exercised on the progress of European civilization.

Although it may not be said that Christianity is responsible for the night of ignorance in which Europe wandered for over a thousand years, yet, if not the sole cause, it was the chief and most active agent in the production of that awful catastrophe; and the prejudice then instilled against learning by ecclesiasticism has not yet wholly disappeared. Even in the Reformation which originated in the increase of intelligence, a fanatical crusade against learning was undertaken. Sage professors sent their pupils home with the assurance that the Spirit of God would inspire the true believer.

The first century was the flood-tide of Roman intellectual greatness—the age of inimitable poetry, perfected history, and diligent love of philosophy. Probably at no period in the history of the ancient world did the masses enjoy in a higher degree the comforts of life. The refinement of the few reached to the many, and the love of knowledge was not a monopoly of a select circle. The age immediately following yielded historians, lawyers, and philosophers, who would have been illustrious in any period, and learning became so generally diffused that there were a greater number of cultivated minds than even in the Golden Era.

The third century presents a different picture. Learning everywhere despised, history degraded to lying chronicles, poetry and philosophy contemptible, and the Latin tongue corrupted into a barbarous jargon. The laws of Constantine and succeeding emperors in the next century could not stay the tide of ignorance. Great men are evolved by the progress of events, not created by laws.

Why this rapid decline from the pinnacle of greatness, in two centuries, to the abyss of ignorance? Not the inundation of Northern hordes so much as the religion introduced into the Roman world during those centuries. The early Christians stigmatized learning as profane, and so identified was ancient literature with the old form of worship that it was held in abhorrence by the fanatical devotees of the Nazarene. In 398 the Council of Carthage forbade its being read by bishops, and the ignorant masses were prevented from incurring the sin by inability. All physical sciences were held as impious and inconsistent with revelation.

So long as the Christians were an insignificant sect, the influence of their contempt for literature and learning had little effect; but when they gained power and controlled the Government, their influence was exceedingly great. The offices of instructors of the Imperial family and of the sons of distinguished men in the nation, previously held by noble philosophers, were consigned to ignorant and superstitious priests. The knowledge of the Pagan world was discarded, and the dogmas of theology supplied their place. The Church absorbed all the mental activity of the times. Philosophy, poetry, and profane history were discarded as unworthy the attention of regenerated mortals. A new arena was opened for intellectual contest—one which engaged the thought of the centuries. This was polemics; the solution of incomprehensible dogmas by never-ending verbal warfare.

As science expands the faculties and ennobles the life, so such disputations narrow the mind, dwarf its powers, and make it imbecile. These studies of questions which are merely artificial formulas having no existence except in imagination, corrupt irretrievably the fountains of knowledge. While the supporters of conflicting creeds, dogmas, and vagaries disputed, the Latin tongue became so corrupted that the record of ancient knowledge was sealed except to the learned. With the temples ruthlessly destroyed by those who considered them profane, perished the Old Empire of Thought. The heated disputants over vacuities furnished instead their interminable discussions, which, by preoccupying the attention of those who cared to think, excluded the old literature; ignorance became canonized. No adequate conception can be formed of the darkness of the human intellect at this period. Superstition grew like a rank and pestilent weed, and asceticism depressed the understanding to still lower depths. The Old was cast aside, and the literature given instead was valueless. Even the minds of thinkers were led astray along paths beginning in ignorance and ending nowhere. Worthless, except as a curiosity, is the literature succeeding the age of inspiration, when bishops sat in solemn council over such vast problems as the immaculate conception, the manner of the operation of Christ's will, the digestion of communion bread and wine, and the possession of property by Christ.

When the Barbarians overspread the empire, they were plastic as children in the hands of the priests, and were easily persuaded to substitute the Mother of God and Christ for their peculiar deities. The New Religion held high carnival. Ignorance is the primeval slime out of which infallible authority grows sleek and powerful. The Christian hierarchy grew from century to century, grasping power by every possible means, staying its hand at no crime, pausing at no cruelty, until it seemed that Europe must inevitably become a theocracy like that of ancient Egypt, or of the Druids. From commutation, or payment for pardons, from tithes, from share of intestate estates, from legacies, the Church at one time owned the title deeds of a greater portion of the lands of Europe; kings and emperors bowed unclad in the porch of the palace of the Popes, who ruled with undisputed despotism over the spiritual domain, and sought in the same manner to seize temporal affairs.

Out of this night Europe emerged. How? By the influence of Christianity? Who, after reviewing this dismal record of crime against humanity, dare assert that the knowledge by which Europe is blessed to-day, and by which she is superior to the hordes of her ancient forests, flowed from Christianity? If the Christian religion is so productive of advancement, why did it not put forth its fruits during the thousand years it held mankind in implicit obedience, and its nod was more potent than the laws of emperors?

Did it foster learning? Countless martyrs at the stake and on the rack, whose only crime was extending human knowledge beyond prescribed limits, cry to the pitying Heavens. For a thousand years it sat on the prostrate form of a great civilization, and attempted to guide the course of events. What were the results? Read the chronicles of the Dark Ages. With blanched face and trembling nerves call up its scenes of fiendishness, where the representatives of this religion, clad with their power by God, wrought the work of fiends incarnate. The morality of Europe sank below that of the Empire even under Nero and Caligula. Morality, manly self-reliance, and nobility of character disappeared as the new religion gained ascendancy. We now witness its blasting effects on Spain, a fossil of the Dark Ages, where the priest is more powerful than the king he faithfully supports. The poison of unquestioning faith entered deep into the vital current of Spanish life and paralyzed the intellect. It is the same faith that supports the Hapsburgs, like evil birds preying on the people, who detest, but dare not move for fear of the terrible power unscrupulously exercised by the priesthood. Napoleon held his throne, and Louis—his villianous shadow—kept his position on the slack rope of French politics by the same aid. Italy—fairest land on which the sun ever shone—became the stronghold of the hydra—a nation of brigands and beggars. The cowled monk and driveling priest are the types of Church perfection.

Who wishes the hierarchy could have succeeded as they hoped, and made the holy faith, descended from the Apostles, and sealed by the blood of martyrs, the triumphant ruler of Europe? When we read the history of its usurpations, its unspeakable crimes, its love of torture, its fiendish cruelty, are we not unspeakably thankful it did not succeed?

The hierarchy fought against a self-reliant people, and the fortune of events was against them. The Crusades not only exposed the fallibility and duplicity of the Church, but foreign contact enlarged the intellectual horizon of Europe. The introduction of the long-buried classics through Arabic channels stimulated the ever-present desire for knowledge. Aristotle, a thousand years forgotten, became the leader in science, and the new civilization began at the identical point where research in accurate knowledge closed with the ancient philosophers. Humanity had passed a long night of pain, to find its efforts the incubus of nightmare, and to resume where, thirty generations before, it surrendered the burden.

CHAPTER VIII.

THE GREAT THEOLOGICAL PROBLEMS.—THE ORIGIN OF EVIL, THE NATURE OF GOD, AND THE FUTURE STATE.

THE ORIGIN OF EVIL.

'Tis not for lack of goodness, man,
The flames of hell are lit;
Hear a whole world's experience
Proclaim—" 'Tis lack of wit."

Ah! sighing over empires wrecked,
And mighty nations cowled in gloom?
Error is mortal and must die,
But Progress rises from its tomb.
EMMA TUTTLE.

THERE is a tendency of the human mind to accept its ignorance of a subject as involving a problem, and after research has shown that what it mistook for profundity was only vacuity, the devotee holds to his opinion with a tenacity inversely proportioned to the nothingness of its cause. At one time Astrology was believed to present problems the solution of which would unravel the grand enigma of the stars in their relation to man. In another age the Philosopher's Stone and Fountain of Youth were as eagerly sought. We now know that Astrology, the Philosopher's Stone, the Fountain of Youth, were not problems but chimeras. In like manner, moral problems have been imagined, and the welfare of man, not only in this life but in the future, made to depend on their solution. These imaginary problems have probably engaged more attention and discussion than those which have a reality.

Of these, the origin of good and evil, redemption, predestination, free-will, and the existence of Satan are examples, each having called forth the keenest thought, and many having served as controversy for ages, yet all actually being names standing for nothing.

Of these, none have received more attention than the existence of evil. Out of it have grown the overshadowing systems of theology, and the wonderful cosmogonies—childish dreams of infantile man—to account for the phenomena of Nature.

Man is placed in a beautiful world, where the grand and inspiring scenes of land and ocean, boundless forests and plains, the stormy grandeur of the sea, the dreary expanse of the prairie, constantly excite activity of thought and profoundest emotions. Nature with bountiful hand spreads happiness and enjoyment on every side. Man plants the grape, the corn, and olive, and genial showers and sunshine mature the harvest. Nature works expressly for him. The uncultured savage is impressed with the presence of a good Deity who governs for the express purpose of bestowing happiness on his children. He is met, however, by counter-phenomena, which it seems impossible to refer to a good being. The sunshine and shower, the abundant harvest, the exhilaration of health are mingled with the rush of storm, with swift lightnings and terrible thunders, prostrating in a moment the labors of centuries of repose; the parching drought withering and destroying the efforts of man; pestilence dark and fearful, and famine preying on friend and foe. There is an antagonism which cannot be referred to one source. There must exist an inferior or equal power delighting in subverting the designs of the good and benevolent one.

This belief is not of a tribe or race, but is common to all

at a given stage of advancement. It is not a question of time, but of development. Although widely differing in the trappings which surround them, there is slight difference in the countless myths of the world. Viewing Nature through his animality, the savage beholds a reflection of himself, and, unbiased by his geographical position or age, has arrived at similar conclusions. He is constantly impressed with this antagonism. Storm and zephyr, sunshine and cloud, health and disease, life and death, speak in unmistakable language, and as fear is stronger than love, the God of Evil receives by far the greater homage. He views with apathy the blessings poured forth by the Good Deity, but becomes frantic with fear and servilely prostrates himself in the dust at the approach of the Evil. Days of sunshine, bounteous harvests, years of health, are effaced by an hour of storm, the failure of a season, or a moment of pain.

Evil is imperfection. We are not to inquire why an allwise, omnipotent Creator did not create perfectly in the beginning; we must accept the fact. Our improvements acknowledge Nature's imperfections. We would destroy noxious weeds, venomous reptiles, and insects, thereby lessening our toil and ensuring the harvest; we would abolish whirlwinds and earthquakes, equalize climates, demolish mountains, fill up rugged places, and drain marshes and lakes. Such to us are physical evils; to other children of Nature they are not. She loves the reptile of the slime as well as the eagle of the crag, and is equally attentive to their wants. She will perfect herself in due season, imperceptibly, without convulsion or revolution, while man must suffer the pains of his imperfect surroundings and organization. Out of this imperfection grew the evils of individual action. The savage, barely able to fashion a bow and spear, as little feels the impress of a higher law as the lion or tiger, and as well might we say to the latter, as it leaps on its victim, " Cease; it is wrong." Both act in accordance with their organization. It is just and honorable for the New Zealander to refresh himself at his cannibal repast according to his standard. The passions being first developed and unguided, there is, previous to the growth of the intellect, a period of great excess. This is overcome by growth, and, one by one, errors none the less necessary for being false are discarded. The mind matures as the limbs of an infant are enabled to walk. Progress is the evolution of inherent qualities. It is not derived from revelation or any foreign source. To understand a revelation there must be answering faculties in man's mind, else it would be unintelligible. A revelation of morals to a totally depraved being would be in an unknown tongue. Man is organically moral, else he could not have a moral idea; and, possessing innate moral capacities, he has no need of a revelation.

The first conception of evil originated in an imperfect knowledge of Nature, and the personification of this imperfect knowledge is the God of Evil.

The attainments of a later age, by indicating its origin, demolish the dogma. If the Good Deity is infinite in benevolence and power, and created everything as pleased him, he could not have created evil. Then, if evil exists, it must be self-existent—a supposition conflicting with the infiniteness of the Good Deity.

Evil is the friction of Nature's activities working for eternal good.

As man advances, he is torn less and less by the thorns against which he is thrust by ignorance, and we realize that the only divine life is that wherein he comprehends Nature and gladly does her bidding.

Evil can only be overcome by growth.

THE NATURE OF GOD.

Each nation believes that its own laws are by far the most excellent. No one, therefore, but a madman would treat such prejudices with contempt.—HERODOTUS.

THE rise and growth of the God-idea has been considered in those chapters treating the subject historically. From the All-God to the One God who rules all is a long and painful journey. The idea was conceived in a false understanding of natural phenomena, and its progress is the application of increasing knowledge. Monotheism, simply substituting one God in place of many, is scarcely removed from Polytheism. Its great advance is made when it shakes off its personality and believes God to be a spiritual essence.

The protean forms which the idea and conception of God have assumed should teach the falsity of the theory that God is revealed to the intuitions. Xerophanes saw the error of supposing man's conception of God a proof of his existence or character. He said, "If horses or lions had hands and should make their deities, they would respectively make a horse and a lion." English theological writers have rarely ventured to attempt the proof of the existence of God by philosophical argument. Kant has shown their insufficiency. The stronghold is in intuition. The reason acknowledges God's existence. But what becomes of this supposition when it is found that whole nations have no idea of God, and when some of the most enlightened men fail to feel his existence? Monotheism is not the end of the series, but it reduces the gods to one. What is his nature?

He is self-existent.

It is said, in argument of the existence of God, that we cannot conceive of creation, with all its designs and adaptations, without a planner, a creator; at the same time it is asserted that we *can* conceive of the self-existence of the designer! Great is the mind that cannot comprehend the lesser but is amply able to grasp the greater! He is of infinite power, wisdom, and love. Are these spiritual abstractions, or are they personified? Necessarily the latter, and every man's conception must be different, as the god of the lion would be a perfect lion. What logically follows? That as our ideas of God are projections of ourselves, there can be no certain and true idea of the Divine. We may build an ideal of what God must be, analyzed to his elements. He must be infinite causation, as the cause of all; he must be the controlling mind, yet he cannot reason, for that would imply imperfect consciousness; he cannot be said to foresee, for that implies relations as to time; he cannot be said to have judgment, fancy, comparison, qualities of the finite mind. The primary elements left, by analogies, are being, cause, knowledge, love—each of infinite degree.

Can personality be formed from these? Can they be infinite in a personal being? Well did the learned and pious Dr. Arnold say: "It is only of God in Christ that I can, in my present state of being, conceive anything at all." The abstract God is the Father; the personified God is Christ. The Trinity supplies both the metaphysician and the most sensual mind.

God must be infinite. Man, being finite, can form no conception or idea of him whatever. This is an unavoidable logical conclusion, from the necessity of man's constitution.

But, it is claimed, we cannot understand Nature or ourselves—not even the growth of the humblest flower; shall we therefore cease investigation? The fields of thought thus compared are totally unlike. With matter we deal with finiteness, and pause on the threshold of infinite generalizations. With God there are no finite qualities to seize hold of; his very being and constitution of mind are different from ours, and to us his thoughts cannot be translated.

As children strive to clutch the moon, philosophers and metaphysical theologians have endeavored to grasp the infinite. They have failed because attempting the impossible. The world is little better for all their dogmatical speculations. They are only mental gymnasts, and perform no productive labor.

It is claimed that belief in God is the foundation of all religion. This is true of religion considered as the ceremonial growing out of a belief that God demands respect and reverence from man, but not true of morality. Men have believed in all varieties of gods, or renounced all gods, and yet lived honest, upright, and noble lives. The solution of this vexed problem has no relation to morality, being only interesting to religious schemers, who of course must have a God to carry them forward. While the best of men have held diametrically opposed ideas of a God, or placed such ideas with the indeterminable, the worst and most fiendish of mankind have claimed to understand God perfectly, and have waded in human gore to vindicate their opinions, often sealing their faith by terrible forms of martyrdom.

Let Theology bury its myriad dead, whose bones whiten the plains of the Old World; wait till the pitying showers of heaven wash away the stains of blood, the fagot ceases to smoke, the tears of widows and mothers and helpless children be dried, and a great race of people rise from the dust in which with iron heel it has crushed their spirits, ere it call its worship the religion of love and peace sent to redeem mankind.

Science will go her quiet way, of God neither affirming nor denying. Her only office is to point out errors where they occur. All that the past has furnished in proof of the existence of a Divine Architect she pronounces as the assumption of children grasping at the moon. The vexed so-called problem is not a problem; it is a chimera. She goes forward from facts to the order of facts called law, on to the organization of matter. Here the human mind stands on the threshold of an unknown universe into which it can go, which it will conquer and claim, only to find, as the intellect grows acute, new domains extending beyond. As we pass from matter to law, from law to principle, from principle to attribute far beyond the outermost skirts of space, we may tread the sanctuary of the Supreme Being. What is his nature? Is he personal? Is he an omnipotent spirit? Vain questions! When the intellect enters the sanctuary, all shall be made plain. Until then it must calmly wait, content with investigations it can comprehend. The theologians, who fail even to understand the organization of finite man, and scoff with priestly sneer at the words of accurate knowledge, untrammeled by facts may vault on the wings of discordant fancy, and between the tilts they give each other in religious tournament enlighten the laity as to the being of an Infinite God. When they agree among themselves and produce their facts, Science will readily receive their conclusions. Until that time their beliefs must remain inadmissible hypotheses.

THE FUTURE STATE.

Do right; act justly; love your race; then you will safely close your eyes in sleep when age has settled on your earthly form. No shadow will darken your soul, but peacefully will the internal unfold itself, and you will awake in heaven an angel of light.—THE SAGE.

But my mind—by I know not what secret impulse—was ever raising its views into future ages, strongly persuaded that I should then only begin to live when I ceased to exist in the present world. Indeed, if the soul were not naturally immortal never, surely, would the desire for immortal glory be a passion which always exerts itself with the greatest force in the noblest and most exalted bosoms.—CICERO.

A BELIEF in the immortal existence is perhaps more universal than that in the existence of the gods. There are tribes of men too low to entertain it, but it seems that no high state of advancement is requisite for its rudest form. It is from its lowest to its most perfect state a reflection of the intellectual status of its recipient. The savage passes to a land where the chase is successful, a country stocked with game. They place in the grave of the dead warrior his bow and arrow and provisions for his lonely journey. All go to one place. As man advances, orders of merit are recognized; the good are separated from the bad; either directly or through mediators, the gods pass judgment on mortals.

The doctrine in Hindostan and Egypt early attained a complex expression. The spirit, although immortal and descending from eternity, became involved in the vortex of metempsychosis, and was compelled to follow a weary round of being. The belief has descended to the present in the petrified theology of Hindostan. The visible body contains a subtle invisible body, to which the faculties are assigned. This spiritual body is not cast off at death, but accompanies the soul in its transmigration, until it is left at the beatific absorption into the bosom of Brahm; then it returns, and is again clothed with a physical body, the form of which depends on the character of the soul that last inhabited it.

This expression of the doctrine has been more widely received than any other. It was early transferred to Greece, and appears in the songs of her bards and the speculations of her philosophers. Greece always had her sceptics, but immortality was defended by her best minds. Her philosophers built up metaphysical arguments with similar tact and acumen to that manifested by metaphysical theologians of to-day, and equally well succeeded in asking more questions than they answered. Her poets dreamed of Elysian fields, and her people received their fancies with the same relish they did the lucubrations of her sages. When there are no facts to guide the vaulting imagination, there is no predicting whither it will take its erratic course. The doctrine as prepared by the Grecians was received by the Romans.

The priests early seized the doctrine, and forged out of it chains for the spirit. It gave them not only power over the body, but also enabled them to blast the immortal being. It would be inferred that the chosen people of God from the beginning had a clear and perfect conception of immortal life. As a cardinal doctrine of religion and incentive to morality they should have understood its elements, and their sacred books definitely expressed it. These books indicate their human origin by their conflicting statements of this important subject, at times showing that the writers had a dim idea of futurity, and at others positively denying it. The early writers placed the seat of the soul in the blood, the breath, the heart, and the bowels. Their ideas were fluctuating and indefinite. The future state was a dark, joyless, conscious state, like the shadow-land of the Greek poets. The prophets could be evoked by witches; and favorites of the gods, like Enoch and Elijah, were miraculously translated. Again, the doctrine is positively denied in the Sacred Word. "As the waters fail from the sea, and the flood decayeth and drieth up, so man lieth down and riseth not." &c. "For there is no work, nor device, nor knowledge, nor wisdom in the grave whither thou goest." "For that which befalleth the sons of men befalleth the beasts. . . As the one dieth, so dieth the other; yea, they have all one breath."

During the exile, the Jews imbibed from the religion of Zoroaster a more complete idea of immortality. Henceforth the sacred writers speak more definitely, and in Maccabees a moral application is made. It is used as an incentive. The righteous are to be happy, the sinful miserable, in the next life. At the advent of Jesus we find three phases of the belief entertained by three distinct seets. The Pharisees maintained the resurrection of the body—an idea older than the Egyptian Pyramids. A divergent portion received also the doctrine of transmigration, and must have entertained the companion belief of pre-existence. The Essenes believed in a future state, where the actions of this life would be rewarded or punished, but discarded the corporeal resurrection. The Sadducees were doubters, and entirely discarded the doctrine. Such was the influence of revelation on those for whom it was especially designed.

The advance of the idea of a future state as a reflection of the receiving mind kept pace with intellectual growth. It has been discarded by many great thinkers, and received by other minds equally great, and it would seem that the abilities of metaphysics have been exhausted in the arguments on either side.

The New Testament, as well as the Old, leaves the subject of the *form* of future existence indeterminate. From them certain sects claim the resurrection of the body and its reinhabiting the earth; others the reverse. Some claim the eternal death of the wicked; others their eternal torture.

The belief has been used to terrible account by the priesthood. The ghastly theology of Christianity turns on immortality. Hell and its fearful despot are the stock-in-trade of the Protestant, and praying souls out of purgatory the lucrative business of the Catholic priesthood.

Man having fallen, and thereby committed an infinite sin, must be saved. This theology does not trouble itself about this life, but is vitally concerned with the next. Earthly life is too brief for it to carry out its diabolic schemes of endless torture. Eternal life must be admitted for that purpose. It breaks the continuity of existence at death; what is good for this life may be damnation for the next; overrides all laws, and howls the doom of myriads damned. It is not surprising that culture, disgusted with such barbarous doctrines, should revolt against them and support absolute materialism, finding in that system the true basis of morality and happiness.

Metempsychosis does not meet the scientific demands of an immortal existence. It involves the birth and existence of every living being in direct interference of a personal God, a perpetual miracle. If the spirit clothes itself with flesh through embryonic growth, then it follows that generation itself is only another name for this process, and could not exist without a spirit ready to be incarnated. The science of life in such case would become valueless and visionary. While every fact of science opposes this theory, it has not a single evidence of its own to bring in support. The vague sense of double existence, or a preceding state, to which is given so much weight, is fully explained by the well-determined duality of the brain, both hemispheres normally receiving the same impression at the same instant, and thus combining them as one, as the double organs of seeing and hearing convert two waves or two images into one. But abnormally one hemisphere acts slower than the other. An indeterminate interval of time intervenes between the two actions, and one is projected into the past, confounded with things remembered. The theory is opposed to science, as it breaks the continuity of evolution, and substitutes miracle for law.

As sure as creation is pervaded by a fixed and determinate plan, is it certain that man's future life, whatever its form may be, constitutes a part of that plan. When we survey the realm of causation this unity cannot escape us. All causes and all effects tend in one direction, like the irresistible set of a great current. The evolution of organic life out of the primeval slime, its progress through successive types, ascending step by step the ladder of existence, through molluscs, fishes, reptiles, and mammals, to man, indicate terms in the series of advance. Is man the last term? Shall causation, having reached its limit in him, go no further, or expend itself in making him more and more perfect? Then, to our finite reason, Nature is a failure. The perfection of physical form was reached years ago, and advance has been diverted into the new channels of moral, intellectual, and spiritual life. Only in this direction is unlimited progress possible. Man's immortality thus becomes a part of Nature's plan—the great end and aim of creative energy: not a foreign element introduced at death, nor a supernatural state, but an evolution from physical existence, and amenable to determinate laws.

The future state thus considered is no longer a part of theology, but a portion of knowledge, and its religious and moral bearing is radically changed. What its superstitious inculcation yields has already been noticed. It often has a beautiful effect on the life, but more often in the past became a terrible engine of misery and degradation as it was manipulated by craft and unflinching selfishness. When made a part of accurate knowledge, stripped of supernaturalism, held to the rule of law, reduced to the province of science, and viewed with calm reason, immortality becomes the crowning desire and blessing of human life. Under its best phase, as a religious institution, the future of the righteous was a curse; and Prometheus bound to the rock, with insatiate vultures tearing his vitals, is an appropriate symbol of man forced to accept an immortality of despairing misery or passive inactivity. Ennobled as the goal of physical causation, emerging from the slime of superstition, taking rank with sister sciences, the future life, with its lofty ideality, **reacts with irresistible force on the earthly existence.**

CHAPTER IX.

MAN'S FALL, AND THE CHRISTIAN SCHEME FOR HIS REDEMPTION.

As in Adam all die, so in Christ shall all be made alive.—BIBLE.
There is but one religion, and it can never die.—THEODORE PARKER.

THEOLOGY makes the fundamental assertion that Adam was created directly by God, pronounced perfect, and placed in a perfect world. He had the choice of good and evil, choosing the latter, alienated not only himself but the whole human race from God, corrupted absolutely and irretrievably the fountain of morality, and metamorphosed mankind into the offspring of the Devil, corrupt from the crown of their heads to the soles of their feet. "Ever since the fall of Adam, age has shaken the tree of human life, and the Devil has gathered the fruit into hell."

Man insulted the Infinite by his own free choice, and his punishment is endless death. God's eternal justice knows no mercy; and hence man must suffer the anguish and torture of fire, the gnawing tooth of the undying worm of for ever and ever.

This terrible view of the origin of sin and its portentous consequences, conjured out of the gloomy depths of a diseased and morbid imagination, requires an equally tremendous myth for the redemption of man, the fallen god, the incarnate devil. He of himself is powerless. Utterly, hopelessly depraved, he must rely on the atoning power of something outside of himself for salvation.

Creation had proved a gigantic failure. The highest effort of creative energy was an abortion; and the ultimate spirit for whom all this labor had been expended, instead of rising to the light of God, rushed madly into darkness, and became a slave to Satan, his enemy. Logically, it may be difficult to account for a perfect man in a perfect world overruled by an omnipotent and infinite God falling into sin, but theology passes this abyss on the bridge of mystery.

Man, having fallen, must be saved. The Infinite God had performed his best work, and failed. There was no alternative in this unique spiritual cosmogony but for God to sacrfice himself. An infinite sin had been committed, and an infinite sacrifice only could atone for it. The death and never-ending pain of myriads of men would be as a drop to the ocean of punishment required. God as the only Infinite Being, must suffer.

Placing the doctrine of metempsychosis and the Hebrew idea of the efficacy of animal sacrifices together, both ardently supported by the Pagan world thousands of years before Christ, the ready reception of the divine incarnation of Christ can be understood. The Infinite Spirit descended, and in the person of Christ, by martyrdom, paid the infinite debt. The ledger of Heaven by this act was balanced, and an infinite sum carried over to the credit side. "The blood of Christ," says Jerome, "quenched the flaming sword at the entrance of Paradise." The countless millions of spirits confined in the terrible underworld, or Hades, were released, and the heavens were white with the glitter of their ascending wings. Christ died for us; to him we look for salvation, and if we believe in him, even at the last hour, we are safe. The divinity of Christ reflects on his mother, and it is to be hoped that the idea of incarnation will extend to every child, that they may be regarded as incarnations of Divinity—miraculous conceptions, to mature into perfection.

In this scheme there is no choice. "Whatever is not a duty is a sin." A blind obedience is the only praiseworthy passion of human nature, which is so absolutely corrupt that there is no hope for anyone until he is sure it is dead within him. We can do nothing without sinning; but the more we surrender ourselves to God, the less sin we commit. Dreary doctrines; how they distort the soul! And yet how many think the dwarfed, starved, and pinched specimens treated by this system models of Christian virtue! So are there admirers of the distorted evergreens, trained into the forms of pyramids and animals which disfigure many a lawn, who think them more beautiful than the trees of the forest. The elasticity of the tree can be subdued; it becomes so gnarled it ceases to exist. So the mind can be cramped and stinted until it ceases to rebel; but this is a terrible condition—an imposition and a sham.

These ideas give tone and direction to Christianity. They make it a system to be endured, not of development. It is fitly represented as a grievous cross, and Bunyan's "Pilgrim's Progress" is the most popular, because the most correct, picture of Christian life.

If the idea of atonement for sin through the sufferings of another were not so generally received, its refutation might be considered a gratuitous task. Really no belief is so abiding, none more zealously held. Beliefs once thoroughly impressed are well-nigh indelible. The young mind finds a system ready-made, which it is taught to revere, to receive unquestioningly, and which becomes a shell, hard, indurated, impenetrable, from which it is difficult to escape, and in which it is comfortable to reside. Selfishness is strongly enlisted. We throw our transgressions on the shoulders of another, and are saved by faith. The incentives are of the basest—hope of gain and fear of suffering. Heaven is held out by the Infinite Father as a sugar-plum, and hell yawns to frighten! A strange moral government of the world! Can the Church advance out of it? Mankind assuredly can and will, but the Church cannot, for as soon as it does its character is wholly changed. There is no need of a church except to save man in this manner. And man's salvation in this manner is of doubtful benefit. The pages of heathen records present no scheme for more immoral tendency than vicarious atonement. Let the example of the great Constantine illustrate. To none does the Church turn with greater reverence. He was ordained to lead her to victory over the allied powers of the Pagan world. To him was presented the miraculous sign of the cross above the noonday sun inscribed with these words: *In Hoc Signo Vinces*—"By this sign shalt thou conquer,"— and to him on the following night Christ himself appeared with the same emblem and told him to inscribe it on his banners. By the Greek he is worshiped as a saint and called equal to the apostles.

Such is the glass given by the historians of a victorious party, but history truthfully recorded things in quite another light over the character of the imperial saint. The death of Maximian may be excused by the custom of tyrants, and perhaps the betrayal of the trust of Licinius, his vanquished brother-in-law, may be passed over in the same manner, cruel and dastardly though it may be, but the apologis must stand aghast over the inhuman murder of Crispus, his first son, whose only crime was too great a popularity gained in defense of his country. He presents the spectacle of a father stimulating informers against his own son, because that son was a worthy representative of Roman manhood at its best estate; a father listening, countenancing and seizing the opportunity there to assasinate his own offspring. From this frightful tragedy he ran swiftly to other scenes of unmentionable carnage and lust. After a conjugal union of twenty years he condemned his second wife, Fausta, to be suffocated in a hot bath, which had been extraordinarily heated. If so implacable with his nearest kin, that he should have raged like a ravenous beast among his friends is not a source of astonishment. He imprisoned his two nephews with the ultimate design of their assassination, a purpose which he accomplished on one, the other, Julian the *Apos'ate*, escaping afterwards to revive the old Roman religion, for a last and unsuccessful struggle against the new Christianity. He is styled the *Apostate* and shamefully vilified by the Church historians, though his austere life and transcendent virtues put to blush the character of one and all of the early Fathers. Educated in prison, fleeing for his life, and seeing his relatives and friends struck down by the tyrant who represented the new religion, he became disgusted at its cruelty and vindictiveness, and reverted to the grand faith and ceremonies of his ancestors.

The same year in which Constantine convened the council of Nice and sat on a low stool amidst the assembled bishops, "listening with patience and speaking with modesty," he most atrociously murdered his innocent son. The Church for which he manifested so much reverence had a sovereign panacea for sin-sick souls. By receiving the sacrament of baptism, all sins were washed away. Yet the crafty tyrant postponed the ceremony to the last. He was the champion of the Church without entering into fullest communion. He purposely omitted this ceremony that he might, at the end of his bloody career, have full atonement granted. The Bishops for whom he sent in his last illness were deeply edified with his contrition when he at last received the rite of baptism, and was fully pardoned.

Well has the great historian of Rome remarked: "Future tyrants were encouraged to believe that the innocent blood that they might shed would be instantly washed away in the waters of regeneration."

If man never fell, if he is a progressive instead of a retrogressive being, the stupendous scheme is an idle tale, and with it atonement, salvation, and numberless minor dogmas become superfluous. Outside of theology or mythology there is no indication of man's fall. Science has not been consulted by bigoted votaries; her followers have pursued their thoughtful way, while the theologians have gone theirs. Theological speculation is the easiest speculation, for it does not require facts, and if incapable of demonstration, is equally invulnerable to refutation by those employing the same weapons. It has been dimly seen that science conflicts with the biblical myths of the creation, and although on one hand theology has sought to reconcile science with itself, the students of the latter have not made any such attempt, rather shrinking from the application of the facts which they well knew were in such irreconcilable opposition. Geology has proved the vast duration of the world, and more dexterous hands than have yet applied themselves to the work must gloss its revelations to make them apparently accord with the Bible.

With the extension of the age of the Earth, the introduction of man is carried into the Past. Beyond the indeterminate period of tradition, the geologist finds an indisputably authentic volume written on tablets of rock by fossil remains. Adam, as the first man, becomes a myth. Before he is said to have been placed in the Garden of Eden, man had inhabited the earth for a vast period of time. That mystic era before the beginning of history, when man existed as the rudest savage, has been divided into the Iron, Bronze, and Stone Ages. Each of these periods represent a vast epoch. Man first used stone weapons; then he discovered bronze; and, lastly, iron. An age previous to, and lower than, stone weapons has been discovered. M. Boucher de Perthes divides the Stone Age into the ground and unground. He says: "We have no knowledge of any savages at present so low that they do not sharpen their weapons by attrition, but the lowest Stone Age presents us examples of this want of sharpening. The implements found in the Post-tertiary, so far, are only chipped rudely into form; they are spear-heads, leaf-shaped instruments, flints chipped to an edge on one side and left unwrought on the other. When the Tasmanian wants an instrument for cutting wood, he takes a stone and breaks an edge, with which he at once proceeds to his work. Similar instruments are found in the drift. The instruments of the drift are less neatly formed by larger chippings than those of the Scandinavian shell heaps, or of America, Besides absence of grinding, the instruments are very rude, a character which gives them important bearing on the history of civilization." The men who used these weapons made by breaking stones to an accidental sharp edge dwelt in caves. Of them Vogt remarks: " The cave man was the rudest of savages. Perhaps there exists at present no race so low. His diet was exclusively flesh. No traces of vegetable food, nor even hooks or nets for capturing fish, have been found. He attacked his prey—like a wild animal—by cunning, speed, strength; and it seems that with his simple stone instruments he mastered the young rhinoceros. He clothed himself with the skins of animals sewed together with sinews by means of needle-shaped bones. His dwelling was a nest or hut, perhaps little better than some anthropoid apes construct. He had no domestic animals; and not until a later period did he domesticate the dog—the first animal he took under his protection." Such is a faithful picture of the European savage—the progenitor of the Anglo-Saxon.

For the last fifty years facts have been constantly produced in support of the vast antiquity of man; but so strong has been theological prejudice that they have either been strenuously denied or ignored. Human fossils have been repeatedly found in such positions and state of preservation that had they belonged to any other animal they would have been at once pronounced true fossils, but, belonging to man, they were at once cast aside as recent. Slowly and patiently scientists have labored and accumulated a mass of facts which now challenge refutation. In no province of investigation has prejudice more absolutely suppressed facts or silenced reason. Theologians make no mention of the mass of evidence daily accumulating, presuming that science and theology have no relation. They will find in the end that this, like all other questions, must be fought on the ground of positive knowledge. The discoveries bearing on man have been condensed in another volume—"Origin and Antiquity of Man;" and the present pages only allow of the general statement of their results. M. Boucher de Perthes, from calculations based on the growth of peat, makes the flint arrows found in the Valley of the Somme, in France, one hundred and twenty thousand years old, and yet to this vast duration must be added the indeterminable period allowed for the formation of the gravel-bed in which they are found. Human fossils are found in Sweden, at least (estimated by Lyell's data of two feet and a half of coast elevation in a century) twenty-seven thousand five hundred years old.

The investigations of Linaut Bey in the Delta of Egypt give certain evidence that man was sufficiently civilized to fashion bricks and pottery forty-one thousand years before the building of the Pyramids. Beneath this civilized state— for man has already made a great advance when he acquires the art of making pottery—lies the savage, or Stone Age, when he posessed only stone arrows and spears, such as the Valley of the Somme has preserved. He dwelt in the midst of a dense wilderness inhabited by colossal beasts, armed only with a rudely broken flint. For what length of time he had previously existed cannot be determined, but he had advanced from the rudest state by a process slow and painful. The more enlightened a people, the more rapid their advancement. Savage tribes remain from age to age apparently without change, so extremely slow is the awakening of their intellectual powers.

The period of time from the flint axe to that of bronze must be extremely long, and still more vast that which stretches into the night of time to the unarmed hairy savage—the primeval man. All this vast duration lies far below the base of the hoary pyramids, which of themselves are scarcely of historic time, reaching back, according to Lepsius's calculations, to within one hundred and twelve years of the Creation according to received chronology.*

From the brutal savage, through the interminable duration of the ages of Stone and Bronze, man advanced into the uncertain light of tradition. Constantly developing his intellectual powers, he slowly and steadily ascended into civilization. Has he ever fallen? He has been too low to fall. Could the savage, all of whose genius was comprised in the art of breaking a stone to a sharp edge, and using it in offense or defense, fall? He could not well be more savage. But when we pass from the Bronze to the Iron Age, we reach the dawn of history, which, century after century, records the accumulation of thought in unbroken advancement.

Ah, Garden of Eden! state of blissful perfection! you are myths—aspirations of the human heart retroverted into the past.

* For the facts corroborating these statements see the works of Lubbock, Steenstrup, Dr. Keller, Sir Charles Lyell, and the linguistic researches of Muller.

CHAPTER X.

MAN'S POSITION—FATE, FREE-WILL. FREE-AGENCY NECESSITY, RESPONSIBILITY.

Morality is based on Anatomy and Physiology.
An individual is the representative of all the conditions by which he is evolved.
Fate is the personification of the constitution of things.

MAN is surrounded by gigantic, terrible forces, over which he has no control, and to avert which his efforts are as unavailing as those of the brutes. He is a child of the elements, an atom thrown up by their collision and concentration as a bubble arises on a stream by conflicting currents. He is more ; he is a bundle of elements which thus united become a centrestance, from which causes emanate as from the elements themselves.

As the elements from which he springs are amenable to unvarying laws—the irrevocable mandate of fate—man, as the result of their union, must be a creature of fate or unchanging law. The anthropomorphic view of the Universe at once dissolves. The elements he seeks to control are masters. Man is a slave, chained, under their perpetual surveillance.

Is this a truth ? Are we bound to the Achillean car, or are we free ? Seemingly we are free. We are gods, willing and doing in perfect freedom. Ah ! this freedom is a delusion—one of the wiles of our masters to cheat us into self-complacency. Not a leaf falls, not a hair of our heads whitens, but a myriad of ages ago it was written in the Book of Fate. Is a tree overturned by the wind ? It was known before a tree existed, and every acorn counted by the recording causes. Every leaf, every insect which feeds on the leaf, every drop of rain, of dew, every flake of snow which has or will fall on those leaves, was known before the earth was evolved from the abnormal ocean.

The human being, physically and mentally matured, is the representative of every law and condition which has ever acted on him or his progenitors, *ad infinitum*. In him they are not only individualized ; they are *centrestantialized*. He exists because of their action ; he is as they have made him. In this sense man is a creature of circumstances. So far as these forces and conditions acted previous to his birth, he is not a free agent, nor is he in his relation to the fixed action of the great forces of Nature. But on the circumstances which surround his maturity he acts by virtue of his inherent selfhood, the resultant of all previous conditions which make up that selfhood. In this view he may be considered free ; for what we call a man is nothing more nor less than the aggregate of forces and conditions, many of which we understand, and many of which we do not understand. He is free, just as his organization, representative of all previous conditions and forces, will allow. This freedom is quite distinct from the dogmatical tenet of free-agency, inasmuch as it regards man's existence as an effect becoming a cause, and not a self-existent cause.

Difference in the primordial or pre-natal conditions has greater influence than those which environ us after birth. These are integral parts of our being. The difference in these conditions makes the individuality of mankind. Were they the same, all men would be identically the same. The permutation of an infinite series of causes never repeats a number in the series. Hence one man is no more to blame for being unlike another than the oak is to blame for being different from the pine, or the leopard for being unlike the antelope on which it preys.

Character found in oak, pine, leopard, or man, alike is the expression of conditions pre-natal and environing. As the acorn treasures all the forces which have developed it into a germ capable of producing an oak, so the child is a treasure of forces which will develop a man, and such a man as this treasury compels. There is another aspect to this subject. The acorn, germinating in a barren soil, strives according to the impulse of the forces by virtue of which it is an acorn to perfect an oak; but hard as it may strive to gather sustenance from the crevices of the rocks, its knotty roots can support little more than a gnarled and blighted stem bearing dwarfish branches. What should have been a tree, lofty and gigantic, is blighted into a pitiful shrub.

The same acorn germinating in a fertile soil, watered by the same showers, refreshed by the same dew, and enjoying the same sunshine and shade, with every condition save one the same, strikes deep roots down into the earth, and on them towers a column-like stem supporting a forest of branches. So the child constantly suffering the pangs of want is dwarfed and distorted, not only physically, but to the centre of its spiritual nature. The same child surrounded by ennobling influences might astonish the world with its genius. Circumstances make the Alexanders, the Napoleons, Platos, Ciceros, the warriors and sages of the world, but they can do nothing without a preëxisting individuality organized in harmony with their requirements.

It was not my choice whether born a serf in Russia, a slave in the swamps of Carolina, or as I am. Had I been born a serf, so far from thinking of fate, I should have a brute instinct for my native cot, and consider my horizon the limits of the world. So of all conditions in which a human being may be placed; they are ever true to the conditions of their position. Ah! then what becomes of poor human accountability? If we are thus creatures of fate, we may make no endeavor of our own, but, like listless Turks sit still and let the world move. This is not a necessary sequence to the doctrine of necessity. Although Nature teaches a clear lesson, it is not sufficiently clear that "those who run can read" rightly. True, an individual may become so imbued with the idea of fate as to consider exertion on his part unnecessary, and remain perfectly passive. The *idea* becomes with him the moving cause. This, however, is a partial view of the subject, leaving out entirely the influence of individual exertion. Man is a *centrestance* as well as a circumstance. The forces concentrated in him react on surrounding conditions. The philosopher, for instance, is born with the capabilities of becoming a philosopher; he is as ignorant at first as the slave child. In actual acquisition both children are alike; but one child has the desire for and capacity to receive knowledge—the other has not. The desire may be strong, yet obstacles oppose with stronger force, and the "mute, inglorious" Newtons fail to rise above the common level. Knowledge is an efficient circumstance of Fate, and furnishes the strongest incentive for exertion.

This question in its broad domain includes the entire doctrine of good and evil, and the measure of man's responsibility.

If we acknowledge—and it is unavoidable—the *necessity* for all that has been, is, and will be, we cannot stray far from a knowledge of the true position. If, on the contrary, we consider ourselves free and independent agents, with such an erroneous guide we cannot avoid going astray. Bound hand and foot by the gigantic forces of Nature, turn which way we will there is no outlet. Yet, are we not footballs, impelled hither and thither as this or that force predominates? The ball is a passive instrument, a mass of matter opposing only the resistance of gravity. Man is a football for the play of the elements, but he, by the concentration of circumstances, becomes more than a circumstance, and therefore reacts on the elemental blows.

Our existence is the resultant of forces and events reaching back to the dawn of time. These events are evolved in us — are united and individualized. Hence we are not *inactive* footballs. The elements strike at us; we parry the blow or bend it to our purpose.

Here lies the deception. We rush abroad in wild freedom, doing as we please; so we flatter ourselves. He is insane who doubts our free-agency. Our ships outride contending billows; the winds are our slaves; fire, fierce and insatiate, our vassal; and the red lightnings of the storm are grasped in the giant hand of man. Such is our vaunt. Is it true? Very true, but not all the truth. I draw no circle prescribing the capacity of the human mind. It is incomprehensible; its dominion is wide, and day by day extending from its pulsating centre; yet how small the area it has conquered to the vast unknown which environs it! How weak its power of resistance to the resistance it meets! Like a man beneath an avalanche, it can assert its might, but the avalanche crushes onward. Man may roll a stone, but the mountain never. The stone which he can turn and the cloud-capped mountain hold like comparison, as the realm—wherein, by virtue of his centrestantial qualities, he is free—holds to the surrounding province which rules him adamantinely.

In this small realm, wherein we are apparently free, lies the fallacy of our free-agency. Here, too, originated the primitive conception of our responsibility for our actions. This we know: free or not, we are held responsible. Whether we act from choice or direct compulsion, knowingly or unknowingly, we bear the consequences. Is this doubted?

Take an individual at random from the mass. He is as he is, not from his own choice. He is the culmination of a line of progenitors, of the infinite number of conditions in which it is possible for him to be placed. Let us take extremes—one very good, one very bad. Born with an inharmonious organization, possessing depraved passions and insatiate lusts cultivated by his ancestors and poured down to him in a corrupting sewer of slimy filth, he matures not into manhood, but into a beast. All the noble qualities of his mind are crushed and blighted, and he lives only for sensual pleasures. A born robber or murderer, he has all the ferocity and cunning of the wild beast. Miscreated are such ; cast into the world like rude, half-finished pottery. As much to blame the wind for blowing, as much sinful the tiger devouring the kid, as they. Yet Nature holds them to account, and compels rendition of the last farthing. As inexorable as the artificial law which gibbets the felon, she hangs the offender in the scorching deserts of passion, there to await until appetite has consumed itself by its own fires. Then the higher nature awakes, and guides the torn offender to paths of peace.

The harmoniously born, inheriting from noble ancestors all the qualities the heart cherishes, mature to manhood, and live to perform works of goodness. Blessings fall on such in a perfect stream and are received by them, that thereby better work may be accomplished and still greater blessings fall.

It is glorious to be rightly born ; terrible to be otherwise, and held to the rack for the faults of others. Yet the greater part of man's trangressions are ancestral. Circumstances over which we have as little control as over our unconsulted birth impart new directions. Born in a den of vice and infamy, the individual may, by inherent qualities or central impetus, burst the restraints of villainy, and burn a pure star of light over a sea of corruption. If deficient in these qualities, then the central fires and the external burn in unison, and the lowest Stygian depths of perversion or depravity are reached. Surroundings may correct a disordered organization. If we trace our most evanescent thoughts, we find that they are evoked by surroundings. Fate casts us into the world, caring not whether we awake in a palace or a manger—with a silver spoon or a wooden platter, or without platter or provender at all. Stern, inexorable mother, she forces existence upon us, and then rings the terrible mandate in our ears: "You cannot die; you can suffer; you can enjoy—work."

We are from our germinal beginning strained to this rack of iron, and throughout our existence force sustains the empire thus early usurped. Forced into existence and forced to die, of the limited space between these events how little our control! We cannot command our senses, or prevent the brain from receiving the impressions which they convey.

Man's distribution on the globe holds him under check of iron law. The Southern hemisphere and the Northern torrid zone, or the whole globe south of the tropic of Cancer, has yielded no grand civilization, neither has the Arctic Circle. A narrow belt of country along the Mediterranean Sea, across Europe, and extending into the same latitudes of North America, is the whole area of history. Man outside of this little blot on the map of the globe has done nothing worthy of record. Why, unless mentality is amenable to physical laws? And here we approach the gulf said to separate the moral from the physical man. A careful study will show that no such gulf exists. Physical conditions affect morality and intellect in the measure they do the body. The heat of the torrid enervates; the cold of the frigid produces torpidity. The two extremes are equalized in the temperate. Man having acquired the control of forces, supplying himself with light and heat, breaks the fetters with which Nature binds him. Being enabled to carry the heat and light of the sun with him by means of his knowledge of fire, he penetrates the frozen North. He invents clothing and dwellings, devoting almost his entire energies in overcoming the antagonism of surrounding Nature. If he has free-will, it is in this combat; but even here he engages in the same manner as animals do, there being only a difference in degree. He is as irresistibly impelled as they by motives which originate in his environment or that of his ancestors. Man realizes the feasibility of a dam across a river, and constructs it. He is actuated by motives of advantage ; so is the beaver. There is this difference : shut the beaver in a room, and it will construct a dam across one corner, out of whatever material it can find ; man must realize the advantage to be gained by so doing. The beaver is impelled by blind desire inherited from progenitors ; man, by equally blind thirst for property and power, also inherited from ancestors.

Nationalities are moulded by their geography, and it is not left to individual choice to select race or locality. No choice of Lapp or Finn that they were driven to the most inhospitable climate of Europe, and have become degraded by their stern surroundings ; no fault of the Irish that by oppression they have sunk from the rank of a leading Céltic people to such wretchedness ; or of the Red Indians that they melt away before a more civilized race. "Scientific physiology has no better ascertained fact than that man possesses no innate resistance to change. The moment he leaves his accustomed place of abode to encounter new physical conditions and altered modes of life, that moment his structure commences slowly to change."

Any system of reasoning which severs the constitution of man, placing the dismembered parts under the control of separate systems of government, is fundamentally false. Man, physically, intellectually, and morally, is an indivisible unit, and to be understood correctly must be studied as such.

From a thousand grand paternal sources the stream of our being flows and bends. We sleep when drowsy ; we eat when hungry ; we drink when thirsty. For a moment we may will contrary to the desire, but the next moment the will is paralyzed, and the desire becomes paramount to everything else. Will against sleep closing the eyelids, the gnawings of hunger, the burnings of thirst ? Pretty free-agents are we !

So far Destiny is supreme. We die. Can we control the event ? The suicide is the tool of motives. Thales said life and death were the same ; and when asked why, then, he did not kill himself, he replied that, as living and dying were the same, he had no motive for so doing. Does fever burn us in its furnace, consumption prey on our vitals, or miasm rankle in our veins—can we will them away ? We may acquire a knowledge of their laws, and avert their penalties.

"The only way to govern Nature is to obey her laws." The forces of the external world move in certain channels, in which, if we are placed, we are certainly and directly impelled, but we must not cross the lines. As soon as we depart a hair's-breadth, we meet the rude buffet of the elements. We are bound to this rack of existence until death. Until death ? We cannot die. The soul, like the elements which gave it birth, is immortal.

We readily admit that the elements and the vegetable and animal worlds are impelled by these masters with definite and undeviating certainty ; but we hesitate to admit that we, with our apparently independent will, are thus controlled. In a moment of egotism we ask : "Are we not capable of doing as we please, and are we not responsible for the consequences ? Are we not, like the gods, capable of willing and doing ? Have we not vast and unavoidable responsibilities ?" Pleasing questions to vanity are these, but they apply to the grasshopper as well as the man.

But we arrive at moral considerations. Is there a province here outside of and unamenable to law ? Shall we apply law everywhere else, and leave this province to the wild caprice of the individual ? The statistics of the world show the unflinching supremacy of order here as elsewhere. The number and atrocity of crimes vary with the season, and the age of the criminals, with mathematical certainty. The seeming irregularity of individual phenomena confuses the superficial gaze. We cannot say of an individual that he will commit a crime, but we know that of a certain number of individuals one each year will commit a given crime; for, extended over a sufficient length of time, the force impelling to crime is an invariable quantity.

Even the mistakes of men are controlled by laws dimly seen in gathered statistics.

To the grand sum of Nature our individualities are nothing. To obtain the truth we must look to the eternal, and not to the evanescent flashes of the hour. Human pleasures, passions, wants, emotions, are fleeting expressions, and valueless except as they direct us to the constant, the inexorable law.

Of the brute we expect brute actions. What shall we expect of the man with the organization of the brute? We cannot avoid the conclusion that, whatever be the relations of spirit and brain, the manifestations of mind are dependent on organization. Anatomists have remarked the approach of the idiotic brain to that of the lower animals. The brains of savage peoples—Indians, negroes, &c.—approach those of the Caucasian infants. These facts point unerringly to the supremacy of law in the moral and intellectual worlds. We are accountable, but not in the manner we are to artificial laws. We are accountable to laws which form an integral part of our constitution, and to none other. We cannot move in channels other than those marked out by the laws of our nature without pain.

By the possession of intellect we are removed above the realm of brutal desires.

CHAPTER XI.

DUTIES AND OBLIGATIONS OF MAN TO GOD AND TO HIMSELF.

I am satisfied that Cambyses was deprived of his reason; he would not otherwise have disturbed the sanctity of the temples or of established customs.—HERODOTUS.

THEOLOGY claims certain duties which man owes to God. The requirements made at different times have been extremely variable and almost endless. In the early and savage age, man fancied God to be like himself, only more savage and demoniac. His anger was to be appeased ; not his goodness trusted. The best of the harvest and of the flock was set apart for him. The smoke of incense arose from his altars, and the blood of slaughtered victims—too often human—stained his shrine. By this method these child-men believed they best pleased their child-God. After a time the sacrifice is found to become more personal and of higher tone. Whatever is held dear is yielded to the selfishness of God. The world becomes a serpent's den of temptation. God demands everything, and everything must be yielded up to him. He created man for his sole pleasure and profit, and it is man's duty to obey. If he knew the law—as recorded and interpreted by the priest—was God's law, things would be different. Always the priest must stand between us and God. We must drink the water as it percolates through finite channels, often reeking with corruption.

The priest has said : "Thus saith the Lord," and men have run gladly to death. However united they have been

In crushing mankind in ignorance, they have been inconsistent in their interpretation of God's demands. He requires of the Catholic, fasts, feasts, and holy days innumerable; of the Puritan, rest on Sunday; of the Jew, rest on Saturday, and circumcision; of the Moslem, pilgrimages to Mecca; of the Hindoo widow, the burning of herself on her husband's funeral pyre; of the devotee, to plunge into the holy Ganges; of the South Sea islander, to knock out a front tooth or cut off a finger; of a modern Christian, to build churches and make prayers at stated seasons.

To review the various opinions of the different peoples of the world—to see the craft and cunning, the villainy and arrogance of the priesthood, and the ignorance and folly of of the many, presents a sickening picture, from which we turn with disgust. If God has made any revelation of his will regarding the duties man owes to him, he has made it in such a manner that there can be no mistake, nor need of any class of men to act as interpreters.

God knows what man wants, quite as well as the priests, however well educated they may be. With astonishing audacity they place themselves between God and man to make plain what He had not power to render intelligible. God's laws need no special interpretation, but are as far-reaching as space, and ubiquitous in their operation. If He makes demands, the mortal need not fear the demand will be unsatisfied. We can do nothing for God. As finite beings, the sum of all our efforts would count as nought to the Infinite. Ten thousand roasting lambs or ten thousand crucified Christs are all the same to him. He must from his very nature remain the same—impassive and immovable. Our duty performed or neglected only affects ourselves. We can dash ourselves to pieces against a mountain, but the mountain remains unmoved.

Let us at once free ourselves from the old idea that God directly interests himself in mortal affairs and can be reached by prayer. A verbal prayer may seem to refresh the heart, but goes no further. God will not turn aside though the whole world cry "Turn." The supposition that He will is a superstition descended from Fetish-worshiping savages. We come in direct contact with laws unswerving and adamantine. They prescribe our duty, which is implicit obedience. All outside and extraneous observances are absolute folly. When the law has been complied with, duty has been done. No fasting, prayer, or Sunday sermon is required.

Duty to God, in the sense taught by the priesthood, is meaningless, except as it gives them an interpreter's position and pay. Ceremonies, observances, and customs made and kept because God is supposed to demand them, are worse than follies—they are infantile stupidities.

Duty! In that one name more crime has been committed, more misery created, than in any other. All the persecutions of the world have been carried forward to compel man to obey God. Jesus was nailed to the cross that the Jews might not fail in their time-honored temple-worship; and the petty churches of to-day wrangle and would crucify each other remorselessly for rejection of their peculiar views. Little cares the Infinite whether a mortal is sprinkled in the face, plunged in the water, or neither sprinkled nor plunged; whether he works on Saturday or Sunday; whether he circumcises, knocks out a tooth, cuts off a finger, or says grace.

Obedience to God can only mean observance of the laws of our being. The only duty we owe is such obedience; and it is time we cast aside the trappings, the ceremonies, and observances which mislead and divert. Here we cannot mistake our duty. We stand face to face with these laws, and need no priest between them and us. If we obey, we at once reap the reward; if we fail, we at once incur the penalty. If in our extremity our lips utter a prayer, it is from habit acquired in childish days, which we know to be as valueless to help us as the breath which gives it sound. Our obligations to God are not prayer or praise, but the fulfilling of the laws which created and sustains us.

By such conduct shall we please him ? The Christian world answers, "No. God is pleased with lofty spires grandly towering above a vain and thoughtless world, with regular attendance at church, long prayers, and sanctimonious face. He wishes man to do everything for His glory and love of Christ, and He bestows salvation, not because deserved, but as a special favor." In olden times He was pleased with the fattened calf, the firstlings of the flock, and the fragrance of smoking blood and roasting offal.

The flippancy of the priesthood is equaled by their arrogance. They assume to be the only interpreters of God's will, which cannot be written, and can only be learned by contact with Nature. His will is expressed by the term Law, and is co-eternal with matter. There can be no law foreign and unwrought into the constitution of the world, nor can man be held amenable to laws which are not a part and portion of himself. Obedience is from necessity, and not for the "glory of God." Is this church God an Asiatic monarch so jealous that we must bow before his throne servilely to gain his approval ? A God making such a botch of creation that we, his misbegotten, abortive creations, creep to his feet to ask his pardon for his having thus shammed us, of all others is the most loathsome.

"No," cries the soul ; "you please not God by long prayers or ghastly faces, sepulchral tones, or sermons beneath lofty steeples. The Infinite breathes through all Nature, and obedience to his will is our ultimate necessity. The world is beautiful, and man walks therein a beautiful spirit. God is not pleased to have that spirit become a blear-eyed bigot, or this beautiful world viewed through the muddy waters of Fanaticism stirred by the craft and arrogance of a self-nominated priesthood. He is pleased with a well-ordered life."

While it is claimed that religion necessarily embraces morality, morality by no means embraces religion. A man may clearly observe the distinction between right and wrong, walk uprightly, deal honestly, act benevolently, and have an unblemished moral character; but if all this does not result from a sense of love and dependence on God, he is not religious. Doing right because right, and avoiding wrong because wrong, is not sufficient. The action must be based on love and dependence on God. If man possessed an absolute and complete revelation from God for his guidance there would be no reason for disobeying or question of dependence; but, fortunately, the Bible, as interpreted by the thousand wrangling sects it has originated, furnishes no such criterion; and Nature makes no revelation except as yielded by closest research and patient investigation.

Having discovered such laws, it may be asked whether man should obey them because such is the constitution of things, or because of his dependence on God. If from the first cause, he is only moral; if from the latter, he is religious. Here is an entirely artificial distinction. Does God demand servile dependence? If so, is it not strange that only a privileged class have learned this lesson? They, never having come in contact with God, assume to tell what He demands, what will please and what displease Him, and the form of religion He prescribes. If God has made a revelation, it is in harmony with the laws of the world. They, as expressions of his unchanging purpose, are finalities. What more can be required than obedience to them?

We come in contact with fire, and are burned. Henceforth, understanding its nature, we avoid it. Shall we do so to please God, or because of our own preservation? Shall we do right for God's sake or our own—for Christ's sake or for humanity's?

Through trial and suffering we gain an understanding of

our physical, intellectual, and moral relations. If a human father should write a code for the guidance of his children, would he not be better pleased if obedience were given because they considered it right, than because it was his will, to which they servilely yielded? But, it is said in reply, "God's ways are not man's ways." Why, then, *attempt* to reason about our relations to him? Unless God's reason is *like* our reason we can know nothing about his demands. The human father would say, "My son, there is no honor in servile obedience. I am not to be considered. Do right because it is right, and you will please me more than by the most slavish submission simply because it is your father's will."

Has God more self-consciousness and vanity than man? Can He be flattered by the "sense of dependence" on man?

The value of this "sense of dependence" and the true position of the "religious element inherent in man" have been shown in the first chapter, and are proved to be as varying as the geographical locality or color of the race. Salvation is not a gift bestowed out of favor. If we do right, we *earn* and *command* it.

Shall we live for the glory of God? Nay, for our own. The Infinite cannot be glorified.

If the order of Nature is unchangeable, of what avail is prayer? Apollonius, who was not enlightened by the mysteries of Christian revelation, truthfully said of prayer: "A man may worship the Deity far more truly than other mortals, though he neither sacrifice animals nor consecrate any outward thing to that God whom we call the First. . . Pure spirit, the most beautiful portion of our being, has no need of external organs to make itself understood by the Omnipresent Essence." Porphyry says of prayer: "It produces a sort of union between the gods and the just, who resemble them." Prayer—the earnest desire of the heart—the prophecy of possibilities—is quite different from the spoken verbiage which a parrot may learn as well. The child, too young to understand the meaning of words, is taught that there is efficacy in a little prayer lisped on retiring. What does it know of the Infinite ? Is there not a striking similarity between the situation of the child lisping a prayer it does not comprehend—addressed to a Being it does not know—and the grave deacon repeating in church-meeting a memorized formula for the thousandth time, praising the forbearance of that unknown Being, and demeaning his sinful self ? How far removed is the pompous preacher reciting his well-learned lesson beseeching God's mercy by rote ? They all think they are doing what is best for them—what their religious education requires ; and are equally self-satisfied as the Red Indian who prays to Quahootze, or the Chinese bowing to his Joss-stick. In some countries written prayers are attached to a wheel turned by water-power, and every minute of the day a prayer is presented to the sky. Who can say that the praying wheel is not as efficacious as the praying parson ? The requirements of prejudice are fulfilled by their several methods. Some striving soul may have found relief in formulated prayer, and thus it came into general use. Some may yet find in it relief. It has become a part of religion. Family service is as essential as church-going, and is the means whereby the theological crust is formed around the young mind, in after years to harden and press out its spiritual energies.

We change nothing by prayer but ourselves. We cannot in the least affect external Nature. If a ship were freighted with a thousand saints, their united prayers would not keep her afloat if there was a plank torn from her side. The Divine Power moves on as heedless of our demands as a locomotive of the school-boy's cry.

If prayer gives us strength and courage, it is well ; but far better the self-reliance of the strong soul depending on no external power.

Nature has no especially holy days, for with her all days are sacred. The learned and exceedingly pious Neander says that "The celebration of Sunday—like that of every festival—was a human institution. Far was it from the Apostles to treat it as a divine command; far from them and from the first Apostolic Church to transfer the laws of the Sabbath to Sunday." Sunday was a Pagan festive day and was adopted by the Christians on that account. The Romans, according to a very ancient custom, named the days of the week after their various deities. The first day was Dies Solis, or the Sun's Day. As Apollo became more popular, the day of his worship was held in greater esteem. Constantine early adopted the Sun as his emblem and Apollo as his protector, and until fifty years of age strictly adhered to their worship. When he was converted to Christianity he would not renounce the day he had always held sacred, and one of the first acts of his reign was to compel its observance. No allusion was made to Christianity in the edict which was prompted by a lingering love of the old religion of the hero gods. The courts were closed on that day except for the manumission of slaves, and military exercises forbidden. The Christian bishops, who saw in the Emperor an incarnate divinity, adopted the day to please their Roman converts. It is a Pagan day devoted to Apollo, or the Sun, and they who keep it in no sense fulfil the command—"Remember the Sabbath day, to keep it holy."

There is no command in the Bible to observe the first day of the week. The old Jewish Fetishism is transferred from the Sabbath to Sunday, and the church-goers of the present think the day far more sacred than any other. Even their house used on that day is sacred. They meet God there more directly than anywhere else. They do not believe the old Pagan notion that He loves incense and the smoke of burnt offerings, but they do believe that He enjoys their praises of him and depreciation of their own worm-like selves. The day is holy, and so strong is this prejudice that the laws for its observance form one of the few instances where religion interferes with affairs of American State. Nature has no Sabbath. The winds blow, the waters run, it rains and is calm, the leaves and flowers expand, the birds sing, on Sunday as well as on all other days. What is wrong on Sunday is wrong on week days; and not until the processes of Nature point out the day of rest should legal enactment seek to make it holy. Until then, Sunday laws are a scandal on civil liberty.

Of faith, it is said it transcends knowledge, and is the only means whereby man's relations to God can be made known. Far more correct to say that faith, the acceptance of authority, has cursed mankind. The more unreasonable and absurd the statement, the more loudly has the receiving faith been extolled. The salvation of the soul has been made to depend on faith, as opposed to reason. Belief depending on reason can be caused only by sufficiency of evidence; it cannot be coerced nor gained by the will. The faith which receives the improbable is attained by narcotizing the reason. But it is claimed that man's eternal welfare depends on his acceptance of certain doctrines. He must believe in God, in Christ, the resurrection, and many other minor dogmas, else he will assuredly be damned.

If he *cannot believe*, what then ? Believing or non-believing is involuntary. One man may have an all-receiving faith without reason to trouble him, while another's reasoning powers are so active that he receives nothing without the closest scrutiny. Is one more blameable than the other ? Faith is a blind guide, and is no criterion of truth. It has, in their time, received a stone, a garlic, a cloud, a bull Apis for gods. The myths of the Olympian Court; the fables of the Incarnation of Brahma in Christna; the revelations of Zoroaster, of Moses, of Mohammed; all religious systems, the world over—unlike in everything else—agree in this; the faith, or, in other words, blind, unquestioning belief of their devotees. When Abelard began to prove theology by reason, he was hushed by the priests, who said if he proved the reasonable by reason, he would reject the unreasonable by the same, and this was by no means admissible.

If Christianity had always made the same demands on faith, it might at least plead consistency. It has not. Forced onward by the growth of the race, it has from age to age been compelled to change its ground. It has required acceptance of miracles, a personal God and Devil, witchcraft, the real presence, eternal punishment, predestination, total depravity, infant damnation, and countless other dogmas which have lived their day, been outgrown, and sunk into oblivion. Yet in the day of each, salvation was made to depend on their acceptance. As faith can only be possessed at the expense of reason, it must always be pernicious, baleful, and blasting. The belief in its necessity, united with the dogma of free-will and free-agency, has worked untold misery and ruin.

Science, on the contrary, demands impartial statements, leaving the judgment free. When mankind reach this firm ground, and are able to give a reason for their beliefs, no doubts will cloud their clear sky, nor will they apostatize. Then they will arrive at an understanding of true holiness and purity, and find the theological standard only a caricature. Not the observance of formulated ceremonies, the saying of long prayers, the keeping of saint's days, makes man holy. The devotee who performs weary pilgrimages to the Ganges to wash away his sins is none the better for his pains. The convert to Christianity goes down into the water for like motives, but comes out none the better. Holiness is nearness and likeness to God—in other words, to perfection. None of these forms bridge the profound gulf. They may have been helps to those who first used them, but are dry and soulless to those who follow. The

Stylite, the hermit, the Flagellant, devoutly sought holiness in their various ways—unwisely sought by faith. The world moved on, and in a better age said of them: "Not, O Stylite, on your pillar's windy summit; not, O hermit, in your lonely cave; not, O Flagellant, in the pangs of lacerated flesh, is the perfection sought by you attained. Beautiful to the eye of Infinite Cause is the pure essence of spiritual life; but equally beautiful the bonds of flesh which hold it to earth. It loves the earthly clay as well as spiritual life."

Holiness and purity begin with the body. Gall in the stomach creates gall in the mind, and the demons of persecution have many a time been unleashed by the fever of indigestion. The olden saint was a crucified wretch, suffering unutterable misery. He had but to show his neck cut to the bone by his hair-cloth shirt to be recognized. Thorns pierced his brow; the lash tore his back; hunger gnawed at his vitals; the world itself sank into indefinite proportions; and the demons of hell ever howled around the soul that thus endeavored to escape.

Purity has been sought by renouncing the world and retiring from its allurements. The rocky cavern, the cell of the monastery, the solitude of forest and desert, all have had their fanatical devotees, who, unable to conquer themselves *in* the world, voluntarily banished themselves out of it. An individual may preserve himself unsullied in the darkness of a cavern simply because untempted. He is no better or worse for that. It is not what a man *does*, but what he *is*. Doing is only a revelation of the inner life.

The spirit touches the material world through and by means of the physical body. Hence physical purity is a condition of spiritual growth, and its perfection the rhythmic harmony of all physical and spiritual functions. It is not bestowed by miracle. The waters of the Ganges or the church fount yield it not. It is an acquirement of struggle. It is the serene calm of a life-time of spiritual dictatorship, wherein all the untoward promptings of menial desires have been subdued by the supreme power of reason.

Holiness is only attainable by obedience to the laws of our being. The Anchorite is as reprehensible as the debauchee. The command is: *not crush, but govern;* the proper subjection of the physical and spiritual by harmonious action.

The saint of the past was known by the marks of self-inflicted physical torture; the saint of the present believes a long face, interminable prayers, and self-sacrifice acceptable to God, entirely forgetful of his body, which may be a whitened sepulchre reeking with corruption. The saint of the future will hold his body as noble as his spirit, and of equal importance. The bravest soul is useless in a corrupted body.

Science resolves faith into accurate knowledge—duty into obedience. Piety, which in its lowest stage is servile reverence and love of God, is exalted to a willing obedience—not because demanded by a Superior Being, but because the requirement of the constitution of things. Religion, if in this new sense that term may be employed, is the ceaseless effort for purity and integrity of being, and harmony with the order of the world.

CHAPTER XII.

THE ULTIMATE OF RELIGIOUS IDEAS.

"Ye are gods, and behold, ye shall die, and the waves be upon you at last.
In the darkness of time, in the deeps of the years, in the changes of things,
Ye shall sleep as slain men sleep, and the world shall forget you for kings."

THE progress of thought is in cycles, and history constantly repeats itself in what may be termed crises. Nearly two thousand years have passed since the dawn of the Christian Era, and we find society again entering a similar plane of organic disruption to that which prostrated the magnificent mythology of the Roman world. The wise Polybius records that it was allowable for writers to enlarge on miracles and fables to promote piety; and Strabo that women and the people generally could only be led to piety by myths and fables. It was an age of organized hypocrisy. The philosophers had no faith in the religion they encouraged in the people. Statesmen employed it as a convenience in the machinery of government. Augurs and priests smiled when they met. Authors ridiculed the legends of the gods to each other, while they wrote in exquisite prose and verse in their favor. The State became disintegrated, from the throne of Cæsar to the hut of the peasant; and hypocrisy so skillfully concealed the decay that no one saw the imminence of change.

After a wide circle, society again repeats this state of things. *It has become an organized hypocrisy.* In the United

States, sixty thousand priests daily teach what their reason declares false. They have grasped the schools ; they manufacture opinion, and throttle the Press. Dare the statesmen, lawyers, physicians, or authors come in collision with public opinion ? Not they. The statesman wants office more than manhood, and joins the rabble to gain votes. He will even attend revivals, and become "converted," if he attain his ends thereby. Although a skeptic at heart, he is a ready tool to enact church-favoring laws. The lawyer seeks credit by owning a pew, and sleeping in it two hours each Sunday. To the physician, to be religious is a fair advertisement. The author, most sensitive to the breath of criticism, finds the popular side yield most honor and profit. The merchant finds a high-priced pew a good investment ; and even the mechanic obtains more constant employment by belonging to some church.

While all detest this tyranny, and loathe themselves for yielding to its pressure, they consent to be slaves to each other. They feel they are hypocrites, but know not how to shake the horrid vampire off; and if they knew they dare not. The honest mechanic would lose his rank ; the merchant's goods would remain on his shelves ; the physician would have no patients, the author no readers ; and this, too, most paradoxically, in the midst of those who at heart believe just as they do, and who secretly honor them for openly avowing their belief. The members of the social fabric mutually consent to live lives of debasing hypocrisy, and to make their conversation unmitigated cant.

Our aim has been to show the baselessness of all extraneous systems of morals and worthlessness of religious opinions, as such, distinct from morality based on intellectuality. To gather up the scattered threads of evidence, the ultimate of our position may be briefly stated :

The ultimate of the God-idea is negation. The savage believes everything is God, and soon arrogantly claims to understand his will and purpose. As he advances in k..owledge and civilization, he distrusts his capability to grasp the infinite, and with his growth in wisdom perceives more and more his weakness. God is invariably a reflection of the mind of the worshiper; and when the worshiper, instead of erecting altars and shrines, and addressing prayers to an ideal being, sets himself at work to purify and render himself divine, the end has been attained.

The Christ-idea, developed from a part of the God-idea—the approach of the Infinite to man through the medium of the flesh—is an imperfect expression of the divinity of man, of the infinite possibilities of his nature, and reaches its end when those great truths are received and embodied in noble and true lives.

Religious ideas are outgrowths of fancied relations between man and God. They rest on the assumption, expressed or understood, that God is a personal being, and interferes with the actions of men and the course of Nature, in whole or in part by miracle. Religious rites and observances can have but two motives—to appease the displeasure or gain the esteem of the gods, or God.

God must be personal to render such intercessions of any avail. The impersonality of the Infinite Cause disposes of all the ceremonies and forms which pass for religion. The moral faculties, which from immemorial ages have been persecuted by superstition, are consigned to the intellect, and man, instead of acting to please God, does right because such is the legitimate requirement of his perfected organization. He walks out of the blighting shadow of ritual and creed—the blind reliance on revelation and its interpreters; casts aside his fear of offended gods and demons, recognizing in himself divine powers which rightly used will lead him to divine ends. He does not determine the right and the true by written revelation, but by knowledge of the constitution of Nature. He is pure and upright, not because it pleases God, but because he has inherent capabilities for purity and nobleness of life.

The observance of the fixed order of his being is the right and true, and the harmony of his life will proclaim the measure of his knowledge and obedience.

Are these highlands of truth to be gained without a struggle? Are mankind to have the clouds of ignorance at once swept away from their mental sky? If so, this grandest of revolutions will be unique. Nay, planted on the impregnable rock of positive knowledge, the warfare will be waged between science and dogmatism, the hoarse bray of ignorance. Here entrenched, it has scorned to do more than defend itself against the moss-troopers of the religious marsh-land—the guerillas and bushrangers of theology. Gathering strength, it may become aggressive. The low cannonading of this struggle is heard in the distance. Rome, most sensitive to feel the popular breath, most quick to prepare for the red-handed struggle she has waged for her whole life against humanity, calls a great Council to reassert her dogmas, and give her strength to flesh her fangs on the first faint sign of rebellion to her rule. The Protestant churches are uniting and drawing tighter the reins of theological government.

On the other side, men arise who dare to think, and—thinking—dare to speak.

Shall we repose our confidence in Truth, and passively await the issue? Truth of itself has no power. Religious barbarism has repeatedly conquered civilization, and set the hand on the dial of progress backward many a weary century of blood. The Truth demands exponents and defenders.

Conservatism finds strength in the ignorant masses, and when we consider how few there are who think correctly, who are reliable in their judgments, unbiased and unprejudiced, we tremble for the cause of mental freedom.

Rationalism, the implacable foe of superstition, is slowly gathering its forces for a final struggle. The various battalions of Churchianity have waged many a hard-fought battle among themselves—have looked upon each other with spiteful hate—for slightest differences of opinion condemned each to a place it is almost profane to mention; but now, under the pressure of the accumulating power of Rationalism, they send their bugle blasts down the gale, calling their scattered hosts together, and wheeling their pliant subjects into line. Old and New School Presbyterians on the right; Episcopalians in the centre; Methodists, Baptists, and scattered divisions of various sects on the left; a picket line of Swedenborgians; while the whole is supported by the solid columns of Roman Catholicism, lumbering on with its heavy ordnance, its racks, gibbets, fagots, and dungeons.

In this contest money is as dross, and life itself is of value only as it purchases freedom. We who have come up out of the black shadow of death, traversing the Golgotha overshadowed by the withering shade of Churchianity; who are drabbled with the slime and ooze cast over us by the serpent-tongue of slander "for Christ's sake"—what are we doing? Allowing our children to travel the same road! Sending them to the Sabbath-school or church, and permitting them to drink at will of the same poisoned fountain! For their sakes, if not for our own, let us strive to make *Rationalism* a power commanding respect. Let us leave them the proud name of independent thinkers, and make it a title of honor.

The battle is no longer waged with the uncertain weapons of theology and metaphysics, but the thinker now wields the Damascus blade of positive knowledge, and the result will be decisive. Infallible authority, antiquity, miracles, saints, martyrs, popes, priests, majorities, dogmas, faiths, consciousness, all the trappings that have hitherto been received as divine, holy and sacred, will perish before the keen flame of what is known, and no more shall blight the expansive spirit, for ever.

What will be the outgrowth of this radical change, brought about by the accumulation of knowledge?

The Church, with its hollow shams, shall perish; but morality, the growth of intellect, freed from gross and perverting idolatry shall achieve a nobility of character unknown before. Faith in the doctrine of vicarious atonement, fear of offending a relentless God, the tortures of hell-fire, the authority of a book or a caste, shall pass away before the certain light of man's true relations and a positive development of morals.

www.ingramcontent.com/pod-product-compliance
Lightning Source LLC
Chambersburg PA
CBHW020055170426
43199CB00009B/287